Ford Times
Favorite Recipes

A Traveler's Guide to Good Eating
at Home and on the Road.

Recipes compiled and tested by Nancy Kennedy
Food Editor, Ford Times Magazine

Volume VII

*Book design and
photographic art direction by*

Patrick W. Barney

Editorial assistance by

Bill Robertson, Kay Savage and Mary Zimmer

Photography by

E K O Studios, Inc., Joseph V. Skierski and Gerald R. Kerran

Food styling and preparation by

Donatha M. Mainguth and Visha Kirchner

Props, backgrounds and food

The Table Setting, *Birmingham, Michigan*
Adler-Schnee, *Troy, Michigan*
The Underground Collector LTD., *Birmingham, Michigan*
The Pointe Peddler, *Grosse Pointe, Michigan*
Jinny's Oxford House Antiques, *Troy, Michigan*
Venetian Slate Co., *Hazel Park, Michigan*
The Tile Stop, *Birmingham, Michigan*
Seafood from Pomeroy's, *West Bloomfield, Michigan*
Meat from The Plum Hollow Market, *Southfield, Michigan*

Foreword

We are pleased to present the seventh in our series of cookbooks — books unique in that they form a bridge between kitchen and highway, being of value both to the cook at home and the motoring traveler. Like the volumes that preceded it, beginning with the first, in 1950, this one draws its material from "Favorite Recipes from Famous Restaurants," a monthly feature of *Ford Times*.

Ford Times Favorite Recipes, Volume VII, differs from the preceding cookbooks. Its page size is larger and its recipes and restaurants more numerous — 371 of the former and 237 of the latter. Each restaurant is illustrated by a painting or photograph, along with explicit directions on how to reach it.

To say that our recipes and restaurants are wide-ranging is to indulge in understatement. We include not only celebrated restaurants in New York, Chicago, New Orleans and San Francisco, but many out-of-the-way places that offer memorable dishes. On one hand we have such basic American food as corn bread, stuffed pork chops, lemon chiffon pie and strawberry shortcake, and on the other more unusual and ethnic items like a cucumber sauce for broiled whitefish, *crêpes Hongroises* and Greek rice pudding. As a bow to contemporary concerns about diet we have a low-calorie salad dressing and vegetable dip.

This new volume proves — as our others have proven — that American food is as diverse as America itself. We don't have a single cuisine, we have dozens of them, based on the variety within the American population. Our food is not only American, it is Chinese, Polish, East Indian, Mexican — it is everything, and all of it derives from the fabulous variety of American ingredients.

Our pleasure in offering *Ford Times Favorite Recipes*, Volume VII, comes in knowing it will add to your enjoyment in the kitchen and in the meals you find in your travels.

The Editors

Contents

Contents

Contents

Ford Times
Favorite Recipes

Northeast

Appetizer Parfait – Fitzwilliam Inn, New Hampshire
Bacon and Spinach Salad with Ma Bell's House Dressing – Ma Bells, New York
Crown Roast of Lamb – The Lemon Tree, Pennsylvania
John's Favorite Cheese Cake – Daffodils, New Hampshire

GRISWOLD INN
Essex, Connecticut • illustration by James Stelma

For over 200 years, this historic inn has been welcoming guests, and in all of those years there have been only five owners. There are 20 guest rooms plus the finest privately owned marine art collection in New England. Lunch and dinner served daily, reservations necessary. Take Exit 69 from the Connecticut Turnpike onto State Highway 9 north to Exit 3, then follow the signs to Essex where the inn is on Main Street.

Breast of Chicken

Bone the meat from 4 plump chicken breasts, being careful not to remove the skin. After the breasts have been boned, cut them into small bite-size pieces. Sauté these pieces in clarified butter, skin side down, turning carefully until they are brown on all sides. Place them on a heated platter to one side. In the same pan, sauté 16 small, canned artichoke hearts until they are brown, remove them to the same heated platter. Then in the same pan add 2 cups sliced mushrooms and sauté until tender, while at the same time adding ½ cup chopped shallots with a few slivers of fresh garlic. When the mushrooms are tender and the shallots transparent, transfer chicken and artichoke hearts to pan. Add 1 cup dry white wine; simmer until the chicken is tender. Remove everything from the juices and thicken with 1 tablespoon of arrowroot or flour and pour over chicken mixture. It is served here with brown rice or bulgar white pilaf. Serves 4.

THE WOODLAWN
Madison, Connecticut • illustration by Thomas Sgouros

Take Exit 59 or 61 from I-95 to reach this delightful New England dining spot at 438 Boston Post Road in the town of Madison. Lunch and dinner are served every day except Monday. Closed on Christmas Day. Fred C. Guelakis is the owner-manager. Reservations advisable.

Greek Rice Pudding

½ cup raw rice	1 cup sugar
2 cups water	1 teaspoon salt
4 cups milk	Cinnamon
4 egg yolks	

Simmer rice in water and milk for about 45 minutes or until mixture becomes thick and rice is soft. Beat egg yolks well with sugar. Gradually stir rice mixture into beaten eggs and sugar and mix well. Return to cooking pan, add salt and cook over low heat about 2 minutes, stirring constantly so that it won't curdle. Pour into individual pudding dishes and sprinkle liberally with cinnamon. Makes 8-10 servings.

THE SEAMEN'S INNE
Mystic, Connecticut • illustration by Thomas Sgouros

This inn, designed in the fashion of a ship captain's house in the 1779-1810 era, is part of the Mystic Seaport, a maritime museum featuring major ships, craft shops and collections of maritime artifacts of the 18th and 19th centuries. There are five dining rooms and a summer dining terrace. The menu runs to traditional New England dishes, and authentic New England clambakes are offered. Lunch and dinner served daily. The Inne is half a mile south of I-95 on Greenmanville Avenue (State Highway 27).

Scallops Polonaise

2 pounds bay scallops	2 tablespoons onion,
8 tablespoons butter	finely chopped

½ cup sifted flour	3 lemons, juice
1 cup chicken stock	Pinch of pepper
1 cup sour cream	3 cups hot buttered rice

Wash scallops thoroughly under running water to remove any sand. Dry scallops on a paper towel. Melt 2 tablespoons butter in an ovenproof dish, sauté scallops and onion for 5 minutes. Remove from heat. In a heavy saucepan melt remaining butter, stir in flour gradually. Add chicken stock and simmer over low heat until thickened. Stir in sour cream and lemon juice. Add pepper, then pour sauce over the scallops and bake at 400° for 10 minutes. Serve over hot rice. Makes 4-6 servings.

EAST SIDE RESTAURANT
New Britain, Connecticut • illustration by W. W. Gallmeyer

German and Italian specialties are on the menu of this friendly family restaurant which has recently been enlarged to include an "Old Heidelberg" dining room. Open for lunch and dinner every day except Monday. Reservations necessary. The address is 131 Dwight Street in downtown New Britain. Take State Highway 72 exit from the Berlin Turnpike (I-5). The William E. Bloethe family is the owner.

Italian Veal and Peppers

½ cup vegetable oil	1 pound mushrooms, sliced
1 clove garlic	
2½ pounds lean veal, cubed	4 cups canned, whole tomatoes
3 cups veal stock (or chicken broth)	2 tablespoons cornstarch, moistened with water
1 teaspoon paprika	1½ ounces Burgundy wine
Salt and white pepper, to taste	
1½ pounds green pepper, in strips	4 cups cooked, buttered rice or medium-wide noodles

Heat oil and garlic clove, add veal cubes and braise together over low heat for about 30 minutes. Add veal stock and simmer until meat is tender. Add paprika, salt, white pepper, pepper strips, mushrooms and tomatoes. Simmer for a few minutes. Remove garlic clove. Then thicken slightly with cornstarch. Finish off with Burgundy wine. Serve over hot rice or noodles. Makes 10 portions.

OLD RIVERTON INN
Riverton, Connecticut • illustration by Richard A. Young

This gracious country inn was built in 1796 as a stagecoach stop and today maintains its Colonial charm combined with modern conveniences. Lunch and dinner served every day except Monday and Tuesday. Overnight accommodations, with complimentary breakfast to houseguests. Reservations appreciated for meals and rooms.

The Inn is on State Highway 20 in Riverton. Closed in January.

Corn Fritters

1½ cups sifted flour	1 egg, beaten
2 teaspoons baking powder	1 tablespoon melted butter
¼ teaspoon salt	Hot fat for frying
¼ cup milk	
1 cup canned whole kernel corn, drained	

Sift dry ingredients together. Mix milk, corn, egg and butter. Add to dry ingredients and mix well. Drop by tablespoonfuls in deep hot fat for 2-3 minutes or until golden brown. Drain on absorbent paper. Serve hot with maple syrup and broiled Canadian bacon slices.

Beef Stroganoff

Cut 1½ pounds of beef tenderloin into strips 1 inch thick. Combine meat with 1 cup beef consommé, 1 cup tomato juice. Season to taste with celery salt, pepper, thyme, tumeric, basil and garlic powder. Stir all together and cook until meat is tender. Thicken with 1 teaspoon arrowroot moistened with water. Serve over hot buttered noodles. Garnish with sour cream, ripe and green olives, strips of pimento and parsley. Serves 4.

HARBOR VIEW RESTAURANT
Stonington, Connecticut • illustration by Don McGovern

The French menu featuring superb food, expertly served, gives this restaurant a reputation for the finest haute cuisine in the area. The owners, Mr. and Mrs. George Turner, are inspired by the cuisine of Brittany which they visit each year in the fall. In line

with the name, diners have a picturesque view of Stonington Harbor where many patrons dock their boats. The decor is handsome with dark paneled walls, candles in hurricane lamps, pewter cutlery and fresh flowers on each table. Lunch and dinner (reservations recommended) are served daily except Tuesday. Located at 60 Water Street; the nearest highways are Interstate 95 and U.S. 1.

Veal Normandy

2 pieces thin sliced veal (4 ounces each)	¼ cup Calvados (apple brandy) or apple jack
1 tablespoon butter	½ cup heavy cream
1 small apple, peeled and cut in 6 pieces	2 to 4 tablespoons applesauce, optional
Flour	Salt and pepper

Pound veal scallops to ¼ to ⅛ inch thick. Heat butter in skillet. Add sliced apple and sauté a few minutes. Dredge veal in flour. Push apple aside and brown meat quickly on both sides. Add warmed brandy, heat and flame. When flame subsides, remove meat to hot plate. Add cream and applesauce. Cook over high heat, stirring until sauce is reduced and medium thick. Season to taste with salt and pepper, adding more cream if necessary. Spoon over meat and serve immediately. Serves 1.

PILOTS GRILL
Bangor, Maine • illustration by Kermit Oliver

Located next to the Bangor International Airport, this restaurant, operated by the Zoidis family, has been a favorite of airport personnel as well as travelers since 1940. Take the Hermon exit from I-95. The restaurant is on U.S. Highway 2, West (Outer Hammond Street). Open every day for lunch and dinner; closed only on Christmas Day.

Baked Halibut au Gratin

18 ounces halibut
6 tablespoons butter
¼ cup flour
1 cup light cream, scalded
⅓ cup dry sherry

1 cup fish stock, scalded
4 tablespoons Parmesan cheese
½ teaspoon seafood seasoning
1½ tablespoons paprika

Cover halibut with salted water and bring to a boil. Boil for 2 minutes. In a separate pan, melt butter and stir in flour until smooth, add scalded cream, sherry and fish stock and stir over heat until smooth. Remove bones and skin from halibut, break fish into large chunks and place in casserole. Sprinkle half of Parmesan cheese and all of seafood seasoning over halibut. Pour cream sauce over halibut and sprinkle with remaining cheese and paprika. Bake in 350° oven for about 15 minutes or until bubbling. Serves 4.

THE CHEECHAKO

Damariscotta, Maine • illustration by Charles Borshanian

"For Goodness Sake" is the motto of the Lawson Aldrich family and they prove it every day from April through October by serving menu items made only from fresh ingredients. Lunch and dinner served; closed Monday. In its lovely location overlooking the water, shore dinners featuring native clams and lobsters share menu honors with other Maine foods, unusual desserts and family specialties plus fine wines and spirits. The name Cheechako stems from an Eskimo word meaning "newcomer" but most of the clientele are repeaters, arriving by boat on the Damariscotta River or via U.S. Highway 1. Don't ask for ketchup — they don't believe in it.

Cheechako Lemon Chiffon Pie

6 eggs, separated
1 cup sugar, divided

½ cup lemon juice
½ teaspoon salt

1¼ tablespoons plain gelatin
¼ cup water

Baked 9-inch pie shell
Whipped cream

Whisk together egg yolks, ½ cup sugar, lemon juice and salt in top of double boiler. Heat over water, stirring until custard forms. Soften gelatin in water, add to custard, remove from heat and let cool. Whisk egg whites until foamy. Continue beating, slowly adding ½ cup sugar until stiff peaks form. Add custard and carefully fold in until mixture is smooth. Pour into baked shell, chill 1½ hours. Top with whipped cream.

THE BLETHEN HOUSE

Dover-Foxcroft, Maine • illustration by Fred Browning

Built in 1844, this charming old inn, owned by Paul Plourde, still retains much of its Victorian flavor. The pleasant bay-windowed dining room is open for breakfast and dinner every day except Sunday. Lunch only served Sunday. Closed on Christmas. Reservations advisable for hotel rooms and meals. The hotel is at 37 Main Street.

Black Bottom Pie

2 cups milk
4 egg yolks
½ cup sugar
1¼ tablespoons cornstarch
Pinch of salt
1½ squares unsweetened chocolate, melted
1 teaspoon vanilla

9-inch graham cracker pie shell
1 tablespoon gelatin
4 egg whites
¼ teaspoon cream of tartar
¼ tablespoon white rum (or vanilla)
½ cup heavy cream, whipped
Chocolate shavings

Scald milk in double boiler. Beat egg yolks slightly, stir in combined sugar, cornstarch and salt. Slowly stir into milk. Return to double boiler, cook 20 minutes, stirring until thin custard coats spoon. To one cup of custard, add melted chocolate and vanilla and pour into pie shell. To remaining custard add gelatin dissolved in 4 tablespoons water. Let this mixture cool but not get too thick. Beat egg whites and cream of tartar together until stiff and fold into custard. Add rum. When chocolate layer in pie shell is set, add remaining custard. Chill until firm. Top with whipped cream and chocolate shavings.

MATTAKEESE WHARF RESTAURANT

Barnstable, Massachusetts • illustration by Ray Houlihan

This waterfront restaurant is not only on the water but over it, built as it is on pilings jutting out into the harbor. This makes for casual and informal dining at harborside with space for boat docking. The menu states that all seafoods are delivered hourly from the fish market on the premises. The owner, Robert Venditti, closes up from October 10 to May 21. Otherwise the restaurant is open daily for lunch and dinner. Take State Highway 6-A to Mill Way to Barnstable Harbor.

Baked Stuffed Shrimp

16 jumbo shrimp	*1 teaspoon lemon juice*
½ cup chopped onion	*1 teaspoon celery salt*
½ cup chopped celery	*Pinch of thyme*
¼ cup butter	*1 pound chopped*
¼ cup sherry	*crabmeat*
1 teaspoon Tabasco	*3 cups fresh bread*
sauce	*crumbs*
1 teaspoon	*¼ cup mayonnaise*
Worcestershire sauce	*Melted butter*

Cut shrimp "butterfly," removing shells but not tails. With sharp knife, slit shrimp halfway down and halfway through rounded back. Remove sand veins,

flatten and place cut side up in shallow pan. Sauté onion and celery in butter. Add sherry, Tabasco, Worcestershire, lemon juice, celery salt, thyme, crabmeat. Simmer 15 minutes, mixing well. Mix in bread crumbs and mayonnaise. Mound stuffing in shrimp hollows. Dribble with melted butter. Add ¼ cup water to pan and bake at 350° for 20 to 25 minutes or until stuffing is lightly browned. Serves 4.

HAWTHORNE INN

Concord, Massachusetts • illustration by Richard A. Young

Across the road from Nathaniel Hawthorne's house, this small family inn has six guest rooms and serves breakfast only. At 462 Lexington Road (State Highway 2A) in historic Concord, it is 19 miles from Boston. Reservations necessary.

Wild Blackberry Turnovers

Dough

¼ cup honey or ½ cup	*2½ cups Cornell Mix*
sugar	*(below)*
½ cup butter	*2 teaspoons baking*
2 eggs	*powder*
1 teaspoon vanilla	*½ teaspoon salt*

Cornell Mix

2½ tablespoons soy flour	*2½ teaspoons wheat*
2½ tablespoons dry milk	*germ*
2½ tablespoons bran	*Enough unbleached*
2½ tablespoons rye flour	*white flour for mix to*
	equal 2½ cups

Cream honey or sugar and butter; beat eggs well into mixture until light. Add vanilla. Sift or mix well Cornell Mix, baking powder and salt; add to butter mixture. Blend until smooth; chill. Preheat oven to 400°. While dough is chilling, make filling.

Filling

1 quart fresh
  blackberries
2 tablespoons melted
  butter
1 teaspoon cinnamon
Sweeten with sugar to
  taste (brown sugar
  may be used)

1 tablespoon flour, for
  thickening
Less than ¼ teaspoon
  nutmeg or lemon
  juice, optional

Combine ingredients and mix well. When dough is stiff enough to be handled, turn out portion onto floured board. Roll out to ¼-inch thick and cut into 1½ dozen 4-inch circles. Place heaping tablespoon of blackberry mixture on front half of circle of dough; fold back half over to form top. Pinch edge firmly; prick top with fork. Dust lightly with sugar and cinnamon. Place on lightly greased cookie sheet and bake until golden, about 15 minutes, at 400°.

COONAMESSETT INN

Falmouth, Massachusetts • illustration by Craig Ridenour

Cordiality and comfort, in the finest New England tradition, are the marks of this 25-year-old resort hotel in the interesting Cape Cod village of Falmouth The dining room is open for breakfast, lunch and dinner every day. Dining reservations taken only on Thanksgiving and Christmas. It is at the corner of Jones Road and Gifford Street. Terence Ryan is the manager.

Haddock Chowder

½ pound butter
2 cups chopped onion
2 bay leaves
2 cups diced raw
  potatoes
2 cups court bouillon
  (seasoned broth)

Salt and pepper, to taste
2 pounds filet of
  haddock
2 cups milk
2 cups light cream

Lightly sauté onions in butter, add bay leaves, potatoes, court bouillon and seasonings. Cook until potatoes are soft, then add haddock. Cover and cook for 10 minutes. Add milk and cream. Bring nearly to boil and serve. Makes 6 portions.

Scalloped Oysters

Roughly crush 1 pound saltine crackers with a rolling pin, then mix well with ¾ pound of melted butter. Put a small amount of cracker crumbs in individual casseroles. Place 6 shucked oysters on top of each. Finish off with remaining cracker crumbs. Bake 15 minutes at 400°. Serves 6.

BISHOP'S RESTAURANT

Lawrence, Massachusetts • illustration by Arless Day

The Abraham Bashara family owns and operates this popular restaurant noted for its Middle Eastern food, steak and lobster. Lunch and dinner served daily; reservations advisable. In the evening there is dancing in the Odah Lounge. The address is 99 Hampshire Street in downtown Lawrence.

Grape Leaf Rolls

100 grape leaves
1 cup raw rice
1½ pounds coarsely
  ground lamb

½ teaspoon each
  pepper, cinnamon,
  allspice
1 tablespoon salt
2 lemons

Wash fresh grape leaves and pour warm water over leaves to soften. (If bottled leaves are used, wash them separately.) Wash and drain rice. Mix rice, lamb, spices, salt and juice of 1 lemon. Place about 1 tablespoon of meat mixture on the veined side of each grape leaf. Spread across in a line, turn in the sides and roll up completely. Line bottom of a baking pan with 3 or 4 grape leaves. Place rolls evenly in layers, criss-crossing each layer. Use an inverted plate to hold rolls down. Add water to cover. Bring to boil on top of stove, then reduce to low heat and cook 20-30 minutes. Add juice of remaining lemon 5 minutes before removing from heat. Serve with yogurt. Makes 8 portions.

WHITE CLIFFS
Northboro, Massachusetts • illustration by Argus Childers

The Tomaiolo brothers converted a beautiful 19th century mansion into a fine dining place at 167 East Main Street (U.S. 20) in downtown Northboro. Dinner served every day, 5 to 10 p.m., except Monday. Sunday dinner served noon to 8 p.m. Reservations necessary for Saturday nights.

Fancy Steak à la Pizzaiola

Olive oil, enough to cover bottom of pan	*1½ cups Italian whole tomatoes, crushed*
1 garlic clove, crushed	*1 teaspoon parsley, chopped*
¼ cup each: fresh sliced mushrooms and green peppers	*Pinch of oregano*
	Salt and pepper, to taste
1 pound sirloin steak	*¼ cup dry red wine*

Combine oil, garlic, mushrooms, peppers and sauté until almost tender at medium heat. Add steak and remaining ingredients. Simmer 5 minutes more for medium rare. Serves 2.

STAGECOACH HILL INN
Sheffield, Massachusetts • illustration by Larry McManus

A century-and-a-half ago this was a convenient stagecoach stop; today it is once more upholding the tradition of friendly New England hospitality, and offers food, lodging and good cheer to the

weary traveler. Located in an excellent year-round sports area, it is only 15 minutes from three ski areas on Mt. Race. Dinner served daily except Wednesday; closed in March.

New England Oyster Pies

½ cup water	*1 tablespoon finely chopped shallots*
½ cup white wine	
7 tablespoons butter, divided	*½ cup sherry*
	½ cup heavy cream
Few sprigs parsley	*Freshly sliced mushrooms*
1 small onion	
1 bay leaf	*1 egg yolk beaten with 1 tablespoon water*
2 pints fresh oysters	
4 tablespoons flour	*Pie pastry*

Combine water, wine, 2 tablespoons butter, parsley, onion and bay leaf in pan and bring to boiling. Rinse oysters, drain well and add to wine mixture. Cook gently until oysters are just tender, or until edges begin to curl, about 4 minutes. Remove oysters, strain broth and set aside. Make a white sauce by melting 4 tablespoons butter in saucepan, add 4 tablespoons flour and cook slowly until flour starts to turn golden. Add strained broth, season to taste, then cook slowly, stirring until thickened. Melt 1 tablespoon butter, add shallots and sauté until transparent. Add sherry and cook until reduced to almost nothing. Stir in cream and cook until reduced by half. Stir into white sauce and check for seasonings.

Divide the oysters between 4 or 6 small oval pie dishes, top with sliced mushrooms and fill dishes almost to tops with cream sauce. Brush rims of dishes with egg wash, then cover with pastry tops which have been slashed in several places to allow steam to escape. Brush with egg wash and bake in preheated 425° oven about 10 minutes or until crust is brown. Serves 4 to 6.

VINCENT'S STEAK HOUSE
West Springfield, Massachusetts • illustration by Kermit Oliver

For almost a quarter of a century this colonial tavern steak house has been one of the most popular restaurants in the state. Robert R. Mailhot is general manager and host. Open for lunch Monday through Saturday; dinner served every day. Reservations advisable.It is a quarter-mile south of the Massachusetts Turnpike at 1508 Riverdale.

Beef Stroganoff

12 ounces tenderloin beef, trimmed	1 bay leaf
½ cup seasoned flour	4 ounces Burgundy
3 ounces butter	4 tablespoons tomato paste
½ cup onions, chopped	1 cup brown gravy
2 garlic cloves, chopped	1 cup sour cream
4 ounces mushrooms	1½ cups cooked wide egg noodles

Cut beef in ¾-inch strips and roll in flour. Sauté briskly in butter. When meat begins to brown add onions, garlic, mushrooms and bay leaf. Cook together. Add Burgundy and tomato paste. Let come to boil quickly. Stir gently and constantly. Add brown gravy and simmer about 5 minutes. Stir in sour cream, taste, add additional seasonings, if needed. Serve over hot buttered noodles. Makes 3 portions.

LE COUNTRY RESTAURANT
Williamstown, Massachusetts • illustration by Greta Elgaard

A dining place in the Continental tradition, it is at 101 North Street (U.S. Highway 7), north of Williamstown on the way to Bennington. Lunch served every day except Saturday and Sunday, and dinner every day except Monday. Reservations advisable. Nearby tourist attractions are the

Williamstown Summer Theater and the Sterling and Francine Clark Art Institute. Raymond Canales is the owner and chef.

Chicken Divan

1 frying chicken	4 tablespoons butter
2 cups water	4 tablespoons flour
Salt and pepper	½ cup heavy cream
1 10-ounce package frozen broccoli or bunch of fresh broccoli	3 tablespoons sherry
	½ cup grated Parmesan cheese

Wash chicken. Simmer chicken covered in water with 1 teaspoon salt for 45 minutes or until very tender. Save broth. Remove meat from bones in large pieces, then cut into long slices. Cook broccoli until just tender; drain and place broccoli on a hot, ovenproof shallow casserole. Melt butter in top part of double boiler: stir in flour. Measure 2 cups of chicken broth and stir gradually into butter and flour. Cook over boiling water; when it begins to thicken, add cream and sherry and continue stirring until done. Add salt and pepper, to taste. Cover broccoli with chicken pieces then with sauce. Sprinkle with cheese. Place under broiler until sauce bubbles and is browned lightly. Makes 4 portions.

DAFFODIL'S
Bedford, New Hampshire • illustration by Richard A. Young

About an hour's drive from Boston, this delightful restaurant is on State Highway 101 West, in downtown Bedford. Take 101 west from I-293 just south of Manchester, New Hampshire. Lunch and dinner served every day, except Christmas. Reservations appreciated. John Clover and Rick Loeffler are the owners.

John's Favorite Cheese Cake

Crust

Mix together 1½ cups graham cracker crumbs, ½ cup melted butter and ¼ cup sugar. Press mixture into 10-inch-wide, 2-inch-deep springform pan.

Filling

1½ pounds cream cheese	2 eggs
	¼ cup flour
⅔ cup sugar	1 teaspoon vanilla

Mix cream cheese and sugar together. Beat eggs into mixture, then stir in flour and vanilla. Put into crust and bake at 350° for 30 minutes. Then add topping (below).

Topping

Mix together 1 cup sour cream, 2 tablespoons sugar and 1 teaspoon vanilla and spread on top of hot cheese cake. Bake 5 minutes more at 425°. Refrigerate and, when cooled, top with canned cherry pie filling.

NEW HAMPSHIRE HIGHWAY HOTEL
Concord, New Hampshire • illustration by Guy Danella

This friendly hotel is situated just off Exit 14 of Interstate 93. It is a short run from the White Mountain National Forest and Lake Winnipesaukee. The regal Coach Dining Room in the hotel offers breakfast, lunch and dinner. Overnight accommodations and complete recreation facilities available. Reservations advisable. Matthew Morton is the owner.

Breast of Chicken Eugene

Remove skin and bones from 3 whole chicken breasts. Cut breasts in half and dredge chicken pieces in seasoned flour. Sauté in salad oil over medium heat until golden brown, remove from pan and keep

warm. Heat 6 four-ounce ham slices in oven and then make Supreme Sauce (below).

Supreme Sauce

Melt 3 ounces butter in a saucepan, add 6 tablespoons of flour and cook a few minutes, stirring to a smooth mixture. Add two cups chicken stock and salt and pepper, to taste. Stir in 1 cup warm coffee cream. Strain mixture, then add ½ cup combined chopped sautéed mushrooms and pimentos. To serve place 6 slices of hot toast on individual plates, top with ham slice and a half chicken breast. Ladle Supreme Sauce over each portion. Serves 6.

FITZWILLIAM INN
Fitzwilliam, New Hampshire • illustration by Douglas A. Jones

For year-round fun and relaxation this is one of the few remaining old New England inns catering to the weary traveler by providing food, bed and grog. Located in a tiny village 65 miles from Boston, the Inn continues the tradition of comfort and good food as it has done since 1796. The owners, Barbara and

Charles Wallace, offer fine New England meals, 22 comfortable rooms and summer and winter recreation in a friendly and informal atmosphere. Find it on the Common near State Highways 12 and 119. Breakfast, lunch and dinner served daily.

Pumpkin Bread

4 eggs	2 teaspoons soda
3 cups sugar	1 teaspoon baking
1 cup oil	powder
2 cups canned pumpkin	1½ teaspoons salt
¾ cup water	1 teaspoon cinnamon
4 cups flour	1 teaspoon nutmeg

Beat eggs, gradually beat in sugar. Blend in oil, pumpkin and water. Sift flour with soda, baking powder, salt, cinnamon and nutmeg. Blend into liquid mixture and beat well. Turn into 3 greased loaf pans (8½ x 4½ inches). Bake at 350° about 1 hour or until pick comes out clean. Cool on rack 10 minutes. Turn out and cool completely.

Appetizer Parfait

Place a dab of sour cream in bottom of parfait glasses. Add well-chilled jellied consommé, the red Madrilene variety. Top with another dab of sour cream and place lemon wedge on glass.

HART'S TURKEY FARM RESTAURANT
Meredith, New Hampshire • illustration by Frank Saso

This restaurant features turkey dinners and calls itself "The Restaurant that Turkey Built." Owned and managed by Russell C. Hart, it is located near the junction of U.S. 3 and State Highway 104 at Meredith, New Hampshire. Breakfast, lunch and dinner served daily; closed from December 1 to April 1.

Roast Turkey

Stuffing

⅛ pound of butter	½ teaspoon thyme
2½ cups mixed onion	1½ pounds day-old
and celery, chopped	bread broken into
3 sprigs parsley, minced	pieces
1 teaspoon salt	4 eggs
Dash of pepper	1¼ cups cold water

Melt butter in a pan and sauté onion, celery and parsley together. Add seasonings and mix well, let cool. Stir in broken bread pieces gently. Combine eggs and water and, with a fork, mix into bread mixture, handling as little as possible.

Turkey

Stuff a 14- 16-pound cleaned and fully thawed turkey with the above stuffing. Do not pack tightly. Preheat oven to 300° and place turkey in uncovered roasting pan, breast side down for 3½ hours. Turn turkey over and finish cooking. Total cooking time should be approximately 20 minutes a pound.

PERONA FARMS
Andover, New Jersey • illustration by Raymond F. Houlihan

The third generation of the Perona family owns and operates this country inn that began 60 years ago and has been a boardinghouse and training camp for professional athletes, as well as a favorite restaurant of politicians and theatrical stars. It is in Sussex County on State Highway 517 about 50 miles west of New York City. Open for dinner and Sunday brunch. Overnight accommodations. Closed on Mondays. Reservations advisable.

Stuffed Filet of Lemon Sole

6 9-ounce skinned filets of lemon sole

Crabmeat Stuffing

In 4 tablespoons of butter, sauté 1 medium onion chopped, ½ pound fresh chopped mushrooms, 1 teaspoon minced parsley. Salt, pepper and Ac'cent, to taste. Then add 1½ cups crabmeat to mixture. Butter a 9x12-inch baking dish. Place each filet with de-skinned side up. Spread stuffing over each filet. Roll filet, starting with small end. Hold with skewer or toothpick. Place in baking dish. Sprinkle with ½ cup dry white wine and 2 tablespoons of lemon juice. Dot with butter, then bake at 350° for 20-25 minutes. Serve topped with 2 cups hot Mornay Sauce (a rich cream sauce flavored with freshly grated Parmesan cheese).

PALM COURT

Atlantic City, New Jersey • illustration by Frederick Browning

This elegant dining room is in the Boardwalk Regency Casino Hotel at Arkansas and Pacific avenues adjacent to the famous Boardwalk. Open every weekday for lunch and dinner; lunch not served on Saturday or Sunday. Reservations suggested.

Lemon Cloud Mousse Cake

Crust

Combine 2 cups graham cracker crumbs with 3 ounces melted butter, 3 ounces sugar and 1 teaspoon cinnamon. Place mixture on bottom of 10-inch spring form pan and tap down with a round, flat object. Bake in 350° oven for 5 minutes and cool.

Filling

Beat, at medium speed, 6 whole eggs and 6 yolks until light and fluffy. Add 1 cup sugar and continue to beat until mixture is thick and pale in color. Add grated rind of 3 lemons. Soften 2 tablespoons gelatin in 6 ounces of juice from 3 lemons and stir over hot

water to dissolve, then stir into egg mixture. Place egg mixture in double boiler and cook, stirring until thickened. Remove and cool. Whip 1 quart whipping cream until barely stiff, then gradually add 1 cup powdered sugar, beating until stiff. Add 1 teaspoon vanilla. Fold whipped cream into cooled egg mixture and pour onto crust in spring form pan. Refrigerate for 3 hours before serving. Serves 14 to 16.

TOP O' THE MAST

South Seaside Park, New Jersey • illustration by Don McGovern

Located on a private beach, this shoreside eating place has a great view of the ocean and adjoins Island Beach State Park and the State Bird Sanctuary. The menu offers fresh seafood as well as beef and Continental specialties. Lunch and dinner served daily; reservations not accepted. Take Exit 82 from the Garden State Parkway and proceed to State Highway 37 east over the bay bridge to Seaside Park. It is at 23rd Avenue on the ocean. Ben Nitti is the owner.

Oysters Rockefeller

16 oysters on the half shell	3 tablespoons butter
2 tablespoons Pernod	3 tablespoons flour
⅔ pound raw spinach	¼ pound bacon, chopped in small pieces
1 cup heavy cream	
1 teaspoon fennel seeds	Rock salt
Salt and freshly ground pepper, to taste	

Line oysters on a tray. Sprinkle Pernod on oysters and let marinate. Chop spinach very fine and set aside. Combine heavy cream, fennel seeds, salt and pepper in a sauce pan and heat over a low fire. In the meantime, heat butter in a small sauce pan and stir in flour to make a smooth paste. When cream mixture is hot, pour through a strainer into butter and flour mixture, stirring well. Sauté bacon pieces in a frying pan until light brown, drain off most of fat and add to the spinach. Stir in hot cream sauce and mix well. Cover oysters with spinach mixture and put them onto 4 oven-proof dishes on a tray of rock salt. Bake at 350° for 15 minutes. Makes 4 appetizer servings.

LA GRANGE INN

Babylon, New York • illustration by Richard A. Young

This quaint Long Island hotel opened for business shortly after the Revolutionary War. Lunch and dinner served every day except Tuesday. Reservations advisable. It is located at Higbie Lane and Montauk Highway in West Islip, one mile east of Babylon.

Maryland Crab au Gratin

1½ pounds fresh Maryland back fin lump crab meat, cooked

2 cups Béchamel sauce (white sauce)
¼ cup sherry
¼ cup freshly grated Parmesan cheese

Add sherry to Béchamel sauce and gently fold crab meat into it. Pour mixture into four 12-ounce casserole dishes and top with cheese. Bake in 350° oven until golden brown.

Chocolate Mousse

1 ounce bitter chocolate
6 ounces sweet chocolate
½ cup coffee, brewed
1 cup sugar

4 egg yolks
1 pint whipping cream
Whipped cream and chocolate chips, for garnish

Place chocolate and coffee in a double boiler. Cook until smooth. In an electric blender or mixer beat sugar and egg yolks until smooth. Slowly stir chocolate into egg mixture. Beat heavy cream separately. Fold whipped cream and chocolate mixture together. Pour into 6 champagne glasses and chill. Serve topped with dollops of whipped cream and chocolate chips.

SWISS HUTTE

Hillsdale, New York • illustration by Sam Hageman

In the winter, picture windows in the dining room face the Catamount Ski Area. In the summer the scene is quite different with a brook rushing down the mountain and a natural swimming pool out in front. Any season, the imaginative menu served by hosts Tom and Linda Breen will delight guests. Breakfast, lunch and dinner served daily. Reservations suggested weekends, and during July and August. Closed April and November. Overnight accommodations and vacation facilities.

Roulades de Porc Cordon Bleu

8 pork chops, 5 ounces each — remove bone and fat
16 slices of Swiss cheese
16 slices of prosciutto ham — thinly sliced
6 tablespoons flour

3 whole eggs — whipped and seasoned with salt and pepper
1 cup unseasoned bread crumbs
2 tablespoons oil (more if needed)
2 tablespoons clarified butter

Place pork filets between two sheets of wax paper and pound to ¼ inch in thickness. Alternate 2 slices of cheese and ham on each filet of pork. Roll tightly and skewer with toothpicks. Dredge in flour, dip in egg, and bread slightly in bread crumbs. Heat butter and oil in a 12-inch skillet. Sauté roulades, browning on all sides. Place in 350° oven for 10 minutes. Serves 4.

CAFE DES ARTISTES
New York, New York • illustration by Thomas Sgouros

George Lang restored this famous 60-year-old west side place at 1 West 67th Street, a short walk from Lincoln Center. The atmosphere is informal and friendly, the appointments (including the Howard Chandler Christy murals) charming and reminiscent of the days when the restaurant opened. Chef André Guillou, a Breton, is justly famous for his imaginative menu and superb food. Lunch is served noon until 3 p.m. weekdays, and the same hours for Sunday brunch. Dinner hours are from 5:30 to 11 p.m. every day but Sunday, when they are to 8 p.m. It is closed on most major holidays and for two weeks during late August or early September. Reservations necessary.

Roasted Hazelnut Torte

¾ cup hazelnuts
½ pound unsweetend chocolate
½ pound sweet butter
½ pound sugar

6 egg whites
Pinch salt
Sweetened whipped cream

Roast hazelnuts in preheated 200° oven 10 to 15 minutes. While nuts are still hot, peel off brown skins by rubbing them in a clean towel. Grind nuts to a fine, floury texture. Soften chocolate in top of double boiler over hot water. Let cool. Whip butter with sugar until foamy, then whip in softened chocolate and hazelnut flour. Whip egg whites with salt until very stiff, then carefully fold into the creamed mixture. Spread on buttered and floured baking sheet 17x12 inches. Bake in preheated 375° oven 12 to 15 minutes until top springs back when lightly touched. Cool in pan a few minutes, then invert on towel, remove pan and cool. Cut in 3 layers. Spread mocha filling (below) between layers, on top and around sides. Decorate with sweetened whipped cream if desired.

Mocha Filling

Cook ½ cup sugar and ¼ cup very strong prepared espresso coffee until syrupy, about 3 minutes. Cool slightly, then mix in ¼ pound softened semisweet chocolate, ½ pound butter until smooth. While constantly stirring add 6 egg yolks, one at a time, until filling thickens, over very low heat. Cool.

Seafood Gazpacho, 67th Street Style

5 fresh tomatoes, peeled and seeded
1 sweet pepper, seeded
½ medium onion
1 medium carrot
3 garlic cloves, finely chopped
5 cups tomato juice
⅓ cup red wine vinegar

Salt, white pepper, Tabasco sauce
1 tablespoon olive oil
1 cup small cooked and peeled shrimp
Garnish: Chopped cucumber, chopped scallions, chopped green pepper, chopped dill

Run tomatoes, pepper, onion and carrot through meat grinder or blender. (Rough texture is needed.) Stir in garlic, tomato juice and vinegar. Season to taste with salt, pepper and Tabasco sauce. Whip in olive oil and chill. Add shrimp and adjust taste with pepper and Tabasco. Serve in chilled bowls with garnishes. Serves 6.

THE COTTON PATCH
New York, New York • illustration by Harvey Kidder

A few years ago, a group of transplanted Southern bankers, hungry for down-home vittles, opened what may be the only Southern cuisine emporium in Manhattan. Reservations recommended. At 1068 Second Avenue, between 56th and 57th streets. Closed Monday.

Nancy's Fudge Pecan Pie

Melt 3 squares unsweetened chocolate and ⅓ cup butter or margarine in a double boiler, or in a saucepan over low heat. Remove from heat when melted. Lightly beat together 4 whole eggs, add 2 cups of sugar, ¼ teaspoon salt and 1 teaspoon vanilla. Stir in 1 cup chopped pecans and the chocolate butter mixture. Pour into a 9-inch unbaked pie shell. Top with 1 cup pecan halves. Bake 35-45 minutes at 350°. Pie is done when crust is slightly brown and center somewhat firm when pan is gently moved. (It's better to undercook than overcook.)

THE GRIFFIN
New York, New York • illustration by George Samerjan

Suzanne Pham, the owner, cordially greets guests at this popular East Side restaurant at 313 East 46th Street in the neighborhood of the United Nations. The menu features many Vietnamese-French favorites of Mrs. Pham's native Vietnam. American specialties are also available. Lunch and dinner are served every weekday; dinner only on Saturday. Reservations necessary. Closed on Sunday and August 27 to September 5.

Vietnamese Brochette

1 pound boneless veal	2 teaspoons rice flour
1 pound chicken breasts	3 teaspoons honey
1½ large onions, chopped	1 cup red wine
2 cloves garlic, chopped	6 teaspoons soy sauce
¼ teaspoon Five Spices (a Chinese spice mixture)	24 slices bacon

Cut raw chicken and veal into 1½-inch cubes. Combine remaining ingredients, except bacon, and marinate meat for at least 6 hours. Roll bacon around chicken and veal cubes and arrange on 6 skewers. Place on a tray and bake in a 500° oven for 20 minutes. Baste with marinade. Serve with hot buttered rice and mustard sauce (below). Makes 6 portions.

Mustard Sauce

Combine ½ cup of vinegar with 3 teaspoons dry mustard, 2 tablespoons soy sauce and 1 teaspoon sugar. Blend well.

Salmon Mousse

Combine 1 envelope gelatin, 2 tablespoons lemon juice, ¼ cup boiling water and 1 small onion slice in blender. Blend 1 minute. Add ½ cup mayonnaise, 1 pound cooked and ground fresh salmon, ¼ teaspoon paprika, 2 dashes Tabasco, 1 cup heavy cream and salt to taste. Blend until smooth. Turn into bowl and fold in 1 cup heavy cream, whipped, and 1 teaspoon chopped capers. Pour into mold, chill until firm and serve with Cucumber Sauce (below). Serves 4.

Cucumber Sauce

Sprinkle 1 cup chopped cucumber with 1 teaspoon sugar and ½ teaspoon salt. Let stand 15 minutes and drain. Add to cucumber 1 cup yogurt, ½ teaspoon freshly ground pepper and 1 teaspoon dried mint or dill, crumbled. Refrigerate.

Pecan Pie

Put 2 ounces melted butter in a blender, then add 1¼ cups brown sugar and blend well. Continue blending and add 3 eggs, 2 teaspoons corn syrup and 1 teaspoon vanilla. Grease a 9-inch pie pan with butter, then line with pastry. Cover crust with a half pound of pecan halves. Then pour on blended mixture. Bake in 375° oven for 40-50 minutes or until pastry is brown and filling is set. Cool. Serve topped with whipped cream.

MA BELL'S
New York, New York • illustration by Harvey Kidder

The first restaurant located in historic Shubert Alley in Manhattan (at West 45th Street), this dining saloon offers each table a "Bonnie and Clyde" telephone providing customers phone lines to the outside world. The walls feature blow-ups of famous telephone users with punch line captions. Open 11:30 a.m. to after theatre, every day.

Ma Bell's Bourbon Cheese Spread

Whip 3 ounces Cheddar cheese with 1 ounce of bourbon until it is fluffy. Add a pinch of cayenne pepper. Chill in a pottery crock and serve.

Bacon and Spinach Salad

4 ounces raw, well washed and dried leaf spinach
3 slices crisp, drained bacon
2 mushroom caps, sliced
1 hard-boiled egg, sliced
½ tomato, diced

Combine all ingredients in a salad bowl, mix with House Dressing (below).

Ma Bell's House Dressing

Combine the following: 1½ tablespoons salad oil; 1 tablespoon wine vinegar; 1½ teaspoons chopped onion; ½ teaspoon French Dijon mustard; dash of both Worcestershire sauce and Tabasco sauce; pinch of oregano and salt and pepper, to taste. Mix well. Serves two as a salad course or one for a main course.

OH-HO-SO
New York, New York • illustration by Nils Eklund

Kwong Lum is the owner-manager of this fine Chinese restaurant that boasts an imaginative menu with a couple of dozen dishes served for the first time in Manhattan. Lunch and dinner are served every day; reservations necessary. It is at 395 West Broadway. From the West Side Highway take the Canal street exit, proceed on Canal to West Broadway, then turn left and go three blocks. The Soho art center, galleries and boutiques are in the area.

Honey Prawns

Shell 20 giant shrimp and mix with 1 tablespoon of baking powder. Let stand for 10 minutes, then wash shrimp in cold running water for 10 minutes. Drain well and dry with paper towels. Make a batter by combining 6 ounces flour, 2 eggs and 1 tablespoon vinegar. Mix and beat well. Dip shrimp in batter and fry in 325° corn oil. Serve with sauce (below). Serves 4.

Sauce

Sauté together for 45 minutes ½ peeled orange, 1 large peeled tomato, 2 slices lemon, 2 tablespoons honey, 1 tablespoon soy sauce and 1½ teaspoons vinegar. Stir often. Pour sauce on cooked shrimp and garnish with lychee nuts, loquats and pineapple chunks.

Marinated Steak

Slice 1 pound of flank steak into 2-inch long and 1 inch thick pieces. Slice an onion and combine with steak cubes. Marinate both in mixture of 1 tablespoon cornstarch, 1 tablespoon soy sauce, 1 tablespoon sugar, 1 tablespoon Mei Kirei Len (a Chinese liqueur, or Southern Comfort can be used). Let stand for an hour. Heat frying pan with 2 tablespoons of corn oil at 300°, add 2 cloves of garlic. Fry steak on both sides, turn over in 30 seconds and add 1 sliced onion, 1 tablespoon ketchup and 1 tablespoon Worcestershire sauce. Mix well. Serves 4.

PROOF OF THE PUDDING
New York, New York • illustration by George Samerjan

Labeled "a gem among gems" by many of its regular Manhattan patrons, this restaurant at 1165 First Avenue at 64th Street is noted for quiet elegance and excellent food. Open for lunch and dinner daily under the direction of owner Frank Valenza and executive chef Richard Burns. The menu is sufficiently diversified to please any palate and most wallets.

Steak Diane

This table-cooked steak is a restaurant showpiece. At home an electric skillet can be used with flair.

4 strip steaks, 5 ounces each	¼ pound butter
Dijon mustard	¼ cup chopped parsley
Worcestershire sauce	¼ cup chopped shallots
Salt and pepper	4 ounces Cognac, warmed

Trim and pound steaks very thin. Brush with mustard, lightly sprinkle with Worcestershire and season to taste with salt and pepper. Heat butter in skillet until very hot. Add steaks, sauté about 15 seconds and turn. Add parsley and shallots. Cook for a few seconds. Add warmed Cognac, heat and ignite. When flame dies, remove steaks to serving plate. Simmer sauce a few seconds, pour over steaks and serve immediately. Serves 4.

Lemon Melting Moments

In very cold bowl whip 1 pint heavy cream. As it begins to thicken, gradually add ½ cup superfine sugar, 2 tablespoons sweetened condensed milk, grated rind and juice of 4 lemons. Whip until very thick. Spoon into parfait glasses, chill and top with fresh strawberry. Serves 4 to 6.

NINE DOORS RESTAURANT
Port Jefferson, New York • *illustration by Randall McKissick*

Gracious dining in this unusual old home built in 1803 is the aim of Mr. and Mrs. James Erthein. Guests enter at the street level, order dinner and relax in the lounge bar. When dinner is ready, they are ushered to one of the second floor dining rooms. After the main course, dessert, coffee and after-dinner drinks are served in the paneled library. All this amid fine

paintings and antiques. Open for dinner by reservation every day except Monday. Address 9 Traders Cove near State Highways 25A and harbor.

Rack of Lamb

1 rack of lamb (8 ribs)	¼ teaspoon finely chopped garlic
¼ cup dry white wine	
Juice of 2 lemons	½ teaspoon salt
1 teaspoon rosemary	⅛ teaspoon coarsely ground pepper
½ teaspoon finely chopped shallots	

Have butcher remove chine and feather bones and heavy layer of fat. Between each rib cut down about 1½ inches and chip ½ inch from ends of bones. Place rack in plastic bag. Mix marinade ingredients, pour into bag, press out air, seal and place on flat plate. Refrigerate from 4 days to 1 week, turning occasionally. Remove from marinade, bring to room temperature, then place in shallow pan, fat side up. Place foil on ends of ribs to prevent burning of bones. Roast at 400° about 25 minutes for medium, 20 for rare. (Well done is a crime and not worthy of this dish.) Place paper panties on each rib. Garnish with baked tomatoes and fluted sautéed mushrooms.

SHERWOOD INN
Skaneateles, New York • *illustration by Jim Scancarelli*

In 1807, Isaac Sherwood established this lovely country inn overlooking Lake Skaneateles. Today, after careful remodeling to maintain the original character, it is still operating as an inn and is an historic landmark as well. It is the second oldest inn in New York State. Lunch and dinner served

every day; reservations advisable. Overnight accommodations. Situated on scenic U. S. Highway 20 at the north end of the lake, it is just 17 miles southwest of Syracuse. Take New York Thruway Exit 40 at Weedsport; State Highway 34 to Auburn; left on U.S. 20 to Skaneateles.

Cheese Soufflé

2 cups milk
4 tablespoons flour
4 tablespoons butter
5 large egg yolks
1⅓ cups grated imported
   Swiss cheese

7 egg whites, beaten
   until stiff
¾ teaspoon salt
¼ teaspoon freshly
   ground pepper
Pinch of nutmeg

Warm milk. In a separate saucepan make a roux of butter and flour. Slowly add warm milk, cook until thickened, stirring contantly. Remove from heat, allow to cool slightly, whip in egg yolks and cheese. Add seasoning. Stir in ⅓ of egg whites and fold remainder of whites in carefully. Pour into buttered 8-cup soufflé mold. Place in pre-heated 400° oven on middle rack. Reduce heat to 375° and bake for 35 minutes. Do not open oven door before this. Then check to see that soufflé has risen and is golden. Serve immediately to 8 persons.

PARTRIDGE BERRY INN
Watertown, New York • illustration by Harvey Kidder

William Monnat, a landscape architect, built this charming inn of old barn lumber and beams and furnished it with authentic country antiques. Lunch and dinner served every day, except Monday. Reservations necessary. Closed during January. Three gift shops and a garden store complete the "Garden Village." In November the garden shop features holiday centerpieces, trees and other original designs. From Interstate 81, take State Highway 342

(Exit 48) to State Highway 3, then follow signs to Black River Garden Center and Partridge Berry Inn.

Meat Balls Stroganoff

Combine 1 pound ground beef, 1 small onion, chopped fine; ⅓ cup bread crumbs; ½ teaspoon dried parsley; 1 egg; ½ cup cold water; 1 teaspoon salt and ¼ teaspoon pepper. Form mixture into ½-inch meatballs. Bake in a single layer in a greased baking pan at 375° for 15 minutes to brown. Or brown in a lightly oiled skillet on top of the stove. Keep warm. In a sauce pan melt 2 tablespoons beef fat, add 1½ tablespoons flour, simmer until mixture is light brown, stirring occasionally. Heat 2 cups beef broth and add to browned flour. Whip until smooth. Cook 5 minutes. Add ¼ cup sour cream and 4-ounce can of sliced mushrooms, drained. Pour sauce on meatballs. Serve meatballs over 2 cups of hot buttered noodles. Makes 6 servings.

THE HUNGRY TROUT
Wilmington, New York • illustration by John S. Walsh

The windows of this restaurant open onto the Ausable River, one of the best trout streams in the nation. Located in the Adirondack Forest Reserve, the restaurant offers standard and wild game menus. It is on State Highway 86, nine miles northeast of Lake Placid. Dinner served every day; reservations suggested. William and Joan Lowe are the owner-chefs.

Trout with Golden Shrimp and Sherry Sauce

Melt ¼ cup butter over low heat. Sauté 2 tablespoons grated onion in butter, then add ½ cup flour, mixing to smooth consistency. Add 2 cups whole milk stirring constantly while mixture is thickening. Add: ½ pound

Scalloped Salmon

1 pound can flaked salmon, undrained	1 onion, chopped fine
2 eggs	½ green pepper, chopped fine
1 cup milk	1 cup cracker crumbs

Combine all ingredients and mix well. Spoon into 2-quart casserole. Bake in a 350° oven for 1 hour or more until firm and golden brown. Serves 6.

Raisin Bread Pudding

1 quart scalded milk	1 teaspoon salt
2 cups dry raisin bread, cubed	1 tablespoon vanilla
4 eggs	½ pint whipping cream, whipped
1 cup sugar	

Pour milk over bread. Beat eggs, add sugar, salt and vanilla. Combine ingredients. Mix thoroughly. Pour into buttered 3-quart casserole. Sprinkle lightly with cinnamon. Bake in 300° oven for 45 minutes or until golden brown. Serve hot or cold with whipped cream. Makes 6 portions.

chopped uncooked, cleaned shrimp, ¼ teaspoon curry powder, ¼ teaspoon garlic powder, ¼ teaspoon tarragon, 2 teaspoons Worcestershire sauce, ½ teaspoon Tabasco sauce and ⅛ teaspoon yellow food coloring. Cook mixture over medium heat until shrimp are done, then add ¾ cup pale, dry cocktail sherry, and salt and pepper to taste. Broil six 12-ounce cleaned whole trout (or filleted trout). Serve topped with hot sauce.

HORN OF PLENTY
Butler, Pennsylvania • illustration by Lin Ervine

The central attraction of this restaurant is a 35-foot-long double buffet table which features over 70 hot and cold dishes. Local artists provide changing decorations with paintings for the walls. It is 5 miles north of Interchange 4 of the Pennsylvania Turnpike on State Highway 8, or 13 miles south of Butler. Open for dinner every day except Monday. Groups may make arrangements for special parties.

CONTI CROSS KEYS INN
Doylestown, Pennsylvania • illustration by Harvey Kidder

Since 1758 this delightful country inn has been licensed as a tavern. It is 28 miles north of downtown Philadelphia in the rolling countryside of Bucks County on State Highways 611 and 313 in Doylestown. Open every weekday for lunch and dinner. Reservations advisable on weekends. Closed on Sunday. Walter Conti is the owner-manager.

Soft-Shell Crabs on Toast

Sprinkle 4 soft-shell crabs with salt and pepper to taste and coat them lightly with flour. In a heavy skillet melt 4 tablespoons butter and sauté crabs, shell-side down, for 5 minutes. Turn crabs and sauté them 3 minutes longer. Transfer each crab to a wedge of toast and sprinkle with lemon juice. In another pan heat 4 tablespoons of butter until it turns golden brown. Pour browned butter over crabs and garnish with lemon quarters and clusters of parsley. Serves 2.

Cold Zucchini Salad

Parboil 6 medium zucchini for 3-5 minutes. Cool and slice. Make a dressing by combining 1 minced garlic clove, 1 cup olive oil, 2 cups wine vinegar, ½ cup Gulden's mustard, 1 teaspoon each salt and ground black pepper and 1 tablespoon fresh chopped parsley. Mix dressing well and add zucchini slices to dressing. Chill for 2 hours and serve on bed of lettuce.

MOSELEM SPRINGS INN
Fleetwood, Pennsylvania • illustration by Jim Stelma

Located in the heart of the Pennsylvania Dutch country on U.S. 222 between Reading and Allentown, this charming country inn has been serving travelers for over 120 years. Many dishes are prepared from meats cured in the inn's smoke house. Lunch and dinner served Sunday through Thursday. Closed Friday and Saturday.

Pennsylvania Dutch Potatoes

Boil 6-8 peeled potatoes in salt water until tender. Sauté 1 chopped onion in butter until soft. Drain potatoes and mash using ¾ cup milk. Add sautéed onion, 2 slices cubed white bread, ¼ cup butter, 1 tablespoon flour, 1 egg and 2 tablespoons parsley. Season to taste with salt and pepper. Add another cup milk and whip mixture thoroughly. Place in buttered casserole and bake at 350° for 1 hour. Serves 8-10.

Hot Bacon Dressing

Cut 8 strips of bacon into small pieces and fry until crisp. Combine 1½ cups sugar, 3 teaspoons cornstarch, ½ teaspoon salt and 1 teaspoon dry mustard. To dry ingredients add 1¼ cups water and ½ cup cider vinegar. Pour mixture over undrained fried bacon and cook, stirring constantly until mixture thickens. Use on endive, lettuce, dandelion greens, cucumbers, cabbage or hot slaw.

THE LEMON TREE
McKeesport, Pennsylvania • illustration by Max Altekruse

Jack F. Braun, Certified Executive Chef, was elected United States Chef of the Year for 1977. In addition to presiding over the kitchen at The Lemon Tree, he conducts private gourmet cooking classes at the restaurant. Below are recipe suggestions for festive holiday meals. The restaurant is at 623 Long Run Road (State Highway 48). Take Parkway East from downtown Pittsburgh, exit at Ardmore Boulevard (U.S. 30), go to Route 48 and turn right. Lunch and dinner served weekdays; open until 2 a.m. Closed on Sunday and holidays (except Thanksgiving). Ben Kulasa is the owner-manager.

Hot Crabmeat Canapes

3 tablespoons butter	*1 cup whipping cream*
3 tablespoons flour	*1 egg yolk*
Salt and pepper, to taste	*¼ cup sherry wine*

8 ounces cooked	30 rounds melba toast or
crabmeat, chopped	toasted bread
fine	2 ½ tablespoons grated
	Parmesan cheese

Blend butter, flour, salt and pepper. Gradually add cream over very low heat until mixture thickens, stirring constantly. Briskly stir in egg yolk and sherry. Mix in crabmeat. Top each toast round with the mixture, sprinkle with grated cheese and serve immediately.

Crown Roast of Lamb

5 pound crown roast	2 eggs, beaten
of lamb	½ cup chopped parsley
2 cups celery,	Salt and pepper, to taste
chopped fine	1 teaspoon sage
1 cup onion,	1 cup water
chopped fine	6 red Delicious apples,
½ cup melted butter	cored
1 pound loaf of bread,	¾ cup mint jelly
cut in ½-inch cubes	

Prepare stuffing by first sautéeing celery and onions in the butter until tender. Combine bread, parsley, eggs, celery, onion and seasonings. Mix well, then add enough water to moisten, stirring to desired consistency. Add mixture to center of crown roast, place in 325° oven and roast for about 2½ hours (180°F internal meat temperature) until meat is pink. Bake apples about 30 minutes or until soft. Fill each with mint jelly before serving with the roast.

BLAIR CREEK INN
Mertztown, Pennsylvania • illustration by William R. Boisvenue

Blair Henry is the owner of this friendly country dining establishment, about a 20-minute drive

southwest of Allentown (five miles southwest of the intersection of State Highways 222 and 100). Dinner Tuesday through Saturday from 6 to 10 p.m. Sunday brunch is served 11:30 a.m. to 2:30 p.m. Closed on Monday. Reservations necessary.

Chocolate Cheese Cake

12 ounces semisweet	Pinch of salt
chocolate	2 tablespoons rum or
¼ cup strong coffee	Kahlua
4 large eggs, separated	Graham cracker crust, in
1 cup sugar, divided	a 3-inch deep, 9-inch
1 pound cream cheese,	spring form pan
room temperature	Sweetened whipped
	cream

Melt chocolate and coffee together, stirring constantly. Set aside. Beat egg yolks until they turn a light lemon color, add ½ cup of sugar. Beat until very thick. Add the cream cheese and chocolate to the egg yolks with a mixer at low speed until thoroughly blended. Add salt and liqueur and mix well. Beat egg whites until foamy, adding remaining ½ cup of sugar, slowly. Beat until soft peaks form. Fold mixtures together. Pour into crust. Place on middle shelf of oven and bake at 350° for 1 hour. Turn off oven and allow cake to set in oven until cooled. Then refrigerate for about 4 hours. Remove from pan and top with sweetened whipped cream.

FARINA'S GOLDEN LANTERN
Warwick, Rhode Island • illustration by Arthur Shelstone

This lively restaurant is a home away from home for the stars who appear at the local summer theater and is also a favorite eating place of tourists and natives alike. Ten years ago, when Rose and Al Farina started the dining room, they only seated 90, now they seat over 250. Lunch and dinner served every day;

reservations necessary. Take Exit 117 West from I-95. The address is 1557 Bald Hill Road.

Coquille of Scallops

In a sauce pan combine ¼ cup dry white wine, 4 tablespoons clam juice, 1 teaspoon lemon juice and a dash each of salt and garlic salt. Bring to a boil. Add 12 ounces cleaned bay scallops, reduce heat and simmer for about 5 minutes. With slotted spoon remove scallops and divide among 4 shells. Sauté ½ cup sliced fresh mushrooms lightly in 1 tablespoon butter with ½ avocado, diced. Add dash of salt and 1½ ounces each of white wine and green Chartreuse. To the wine-clam juice mixture add 1 heaping teaspoon of cornstarch dissolved in 2 tablespoons of water and fold in ¼ cup whipping cream. Remove from heat. Combine this sauce with the avocado mixture. Divide remaining raw, sliced avocado among the 4 scallop-filled shells. Pour sauce over shells and sprinkle each lightly with powdered lemon peel, paprika and dill. Bake at 450° for about 8 minutes or until top is lightly browned. Serves 4.

LAURENS
Killington, Vermont • illustration by Richard A. Young

Gracious country dining is the hallmark of this restaurant in an antique-filled 1860 farmhouse. A talented young chef, Francis Clogston, prepares the fine Continental dishes. Dinner only and reservations are a must. Closed Mondays and the month of May. Thomas and Lauren Rabek are the owners and hosts. It is on U.S. 4 in the Sherburne Valley near Killington.

Les Paupiettes de Veau Farcies au Madère

8 3-ounce veal slices, from the leg	¼ teaspoon nutmeg
1 pound ground veal	1 teaspoon salt
2 egg whites, unbeaten	1 teaspoon white pepper
	2 cups whipping cream
2 tablespoons thyme	2 cups Madeira wine
½ cup clarified butter	½ cup freshly chopped parsley
1 cup flour seasoned with salt and pepper	

Trim veal slices and pound to thin pieces about 3x6 inches. Grind trimmings and combine with the ground veal. In a mixing bowl combine ground veal, egg whites, nutmeg, salt and pepper. Whip with an electric mixer on high speed until mixture is thick. Slowly add 2 cups whipping cream to the veal while whipping approximately 2 minutes or until mixture is firm. Add the thyme and mix well. Place pounded veal slices on the counter, spread beaten mixture (forcemeat) over them. Roll veal slices from narrow end and tie gently in the middle. These are now called paupiettes. Heat the clarified butter in a large skillet. Dredge paupiettes in seasoned flour and place in hot skillet turning frequently so that all sides brown. Drain butter from skillet, add Madeira wine and cook over medium heat turning paupiettes on all sides until they feel firm, about 5 minutes. Remove from skillet and reduce sauce, add more wine to this sauce, if desired. Cut and remove string of paupiettes, place on platter, pour sauce over the veal and garnish with freshly chopped parsley. Complement this dish with broccoli florets, hollandaise sauce and rice pilaf. Serves 4.

ROYAL'S HEARTHSIDE
Rutland, Vermont • illustration by Allen Tubach

A native Bostonian, Ernest Royal, who is the chef-owner (shown in the restaurant painting), describes his restaurant's cuisine as "very New England." Gourmets agree that the food is imaginative and the service is excellent. The Hearthside is in a charming century-old inn at the junction of U.S. Highways 7 and 4 in Rutland. Lunch and dinner served every day. Reservations appreciated.

New England Ham and Potato Casserole

1 pound lean, smoked
   ham, sliced ⅛ inch
   thick
1 pound thinly sliced
   potatoes
½ pound thinly sliced
   onions

No. 2½ can tomatoes
⅛ pound butter, melted
½ teaspoon
   Worcestershire sauce
1 bay leaf
Garlic salt and pepper,
   to taste

Butter the bottom of a 3-quart casserole with some of the melted butter. Alternate layers of ham, potatoes, onion, tomatoes and seasonings. Tomatoes should be last ingredient in casserole. Put bay leaf in and pour remaining butter over all. Cover casserole and bake at 375° for 1½ hours. Remove bay leaf before serving. Makes 6 portions.

Heavenly Pudding

½ pound sponge cake or
   plain day-old cake, cut
   into large cubes
½ cup sherry

Soft custard (below)
½ pint whipped cream,
   sweetened

Place cake in a glass bowl and moisten with sherry. Cover the cake and wine with ¾ of the soft custard and stir gently. Smooth the remaining custard over the top of the pudding. With a pastry bag or spatula decorate the top of the pudding with the whipped cream. Chill for 1 hour before serving. Serves 6.

Soft Custard

Beat 4 egg yolks lightly and stir in 1 tablespoon of sugar. Sweeten 2 cups of milk with 1 tablespoon of sugar and then scald milk. Slowly beat the hot milk into the egg mixture. Cook this mixture in a double boiler over the hot water until it thickens, stirring constantly. Remove from heat and continue to stir occasionally until it cools. Add a few drops of lemon and vanilla extract, to taste.

Baked Scallops Hearthside

Butter a casserole and in it arrange 12 ounces sea scallops, sliced in half. Season with salt and pepper and sprinkle 1 ounce of sherry over them. Pour about 2 ounces melted butter over the scallops and cover with 1 cup fresh bread crumbs. Pour additional 2 ounces melted butter over the crumbs. Bake in 375° oven for about 15 minutes. Makes 2 portions. (Alaskan King crab meat or cooked lobster meat may be substituted for scallops.) Serves 2.

THE COMMON MAN
Warren, Vermont • illustration by George Guzzi

An old barn was converted into a delightful restaurant by Mike Ware and Gusti Iten at Warren, in the Sugarbush ski country of Vermont. Dinner is the only meal. Reservations necessary. Closed on Monday and Thanksgiving and Christmas days.

Emmence de Veau à la Zurichoise

2 pounds thinly sliced
   veal leg
4 tablespoons clarified
   butter
3 tablespoons chopped
   shallots
1 pint sliced mushrooms

1 cup dry white wine
½ cup demi-glaze or
   brown sauce
1 cup medium cream
Salt and pepper to taste
2 tablespoons butter

Trim and cut veal into ½-inch strips. Sauté in clarified butter over high heat, coloring well. Remove meat from pan and keep in warm place. Add shallots and cook until transparent. Add mushrooms and sauté lightly. Remove mushrooms and keep warm. Add wine to pan to de-glaze, then add demi-glaze or brown sauce and cook until reduced in half. Stir in cream, season to taste with salt and pepper and simmer gently, reducing liquid to consistency of cream. A small amount of arrowroot may be used to thicken if necessary. Just before serving, return veal and mushrooms to sauce and heat gently without boiling. Stir in butter. Serve with rice or noodles.

Southeast

Chocolate Fondue – Pinehurst Hotel, North Carolina
Pinkie's Shrimp Boil – Calibogue Cafe, South Carolina
Eggplant Antipasto – Sheraton at Sandestin, Florida
Shredded Yams – New Perry Hotel, Georgia

SQUARE RIGGER INN
Fairhope, Alabama • illustration by Don Ross

Nestled under a magnificent century-old oak tree, this charming country inn is famous for its Southern hospitality and excellent seafood and steaks. On scenic U.S. Highway 98, it is 10 miles south of Interstate 10 between Fairhope and Point Clear. Open for lunch and dinner every day except Sunday evening and Monday. Tonya and Joseph Martinez and Elsie and Wallace Milham are the owner-managers.

Seafood Gumbo

2 tablespoons bacon fat	1 teaspoon salt
2½ tablespoons flour	Pepper, to taste
1 cup chopped onions	⅓ cup Worcestershire
1 cup chopped green	sauce
peppers	1 pound raw crabmeat
2 10-ounce packages	½ pound raw cleaned
frozen cut okra	shrimp
1 No. 2 can tomatoes	3 cups hot cooked rice

Make a roux by blending bacon fat and flour. Stir and cook constantly until it is dark brown. *Be careful not to scorch.* Add onions and peppers and sauté until vegetables are soft. Stir in cut okra, tomatoes, seasonings and cook for a few minutes. Add this mixture to 2 quarts of boiling water, stirring in gradually. Add crabmeat and shrimp and let boil for about 1 hour. Serve over hot rice. Makes 6 portions.

TRIANGLE RESTAURANT
Riverview, Alabama • illustration by Fred W. Thomas

This friendly restaurant is about 35 miles south of Calloway Gardens, Georgia, and is seven miles from I-85. Take the Fairfax Exit and proceed to end of road, turning right on State Highway 29. Turn left at State

Highway 87 and proceed four miles to restaurant. Dinner is served every day except Sunday. Bert Sims is the owner.

Beef Kabob

Cook 2 cups of wild rice according to directions, set aside and keep warm. Broil a thick rib-eye steak to desired degree. While steak is broiling, dice into medium-size pieces 1 tomato, ½ green pepper and ½ onion. Sauté vegetables in a skillet. When steak is done, cut into bite-size pieces and stir in with vegetables and cook for a couple of minutes. Spread cooked rice in a serving dish and top with meat and vegetable mixture. Serves 2.

Fried Eggplant

Cut a large eggplant into thin strips about ⅛-inch thick. Soak overnight in kosher salt, lemon juice and cold water. Remove eggplant from marinade, rinse and dip in 1 cup of milk and then lightly coat with self-rising flour. Deep-fry pieces until golden brown. Serves 4.

HOTEL duPONT
Wilmington, Delaware • illustration by Don Odle

There are two fine restaurants in this small, elegant 65-year-old hotel — the Green and Brandywine rooms. The dining rooms are noted for their fine original paintings, including 12 original Wyeths, by three generations of the noted family of artists. One of the most popular items served on the luncheon menu is the Open-Faced Backfin Crab Sandwich. Open for breakfast, lunch and dinner; reservations advisable for meals and overnight accommodations. From Interstate 95, take Exit 7 east on State Highway 52 (Delaware Avenue). Bear left on 11th Street. Proceed three blocks to hotel at 11th and Market Streets.

Open-Faced Crab Sandwich

Take 12 ounces cooked backfin crabmeat and mix it with ¼ teaspoon each of Tabasco, Worcestershire sauce and lemon juice. Then mix in 4 tablespoons of mayonnaise. Toast 8 pieces white bread and spread them with 4 tablespoons tartar sauce. Cover toast with crabmeat mixture and heat broiler. Cover each sandwich with a slice of American or Cheddar cheese, sprinkle with paprika. Place under broiler until cheese melts and is bubbly. Serve piping hot garnished with lemon wedges and parsley. Makes 4 portions.

Longe de Veau Rostoff

Marinate 3 pounds loin of milk-fed veal with juice of 2 lemons, 8 finely chopped shallots, 2 teaspoons dill leaves and 1 teaspoon thyme for 2 hours. Brown both sides quickly and oven-roast at 375° for 40-60 minutes. Remove veal from pan, add veal stock made from veal bones, and reduce to half. Add 3 cups sour cream and remove from heat. Cut 3 slices per person and top with sauce. Serves 8. For garnish cut 4 medium size cucumbers in eighths and shape to ovals like chateau potatoes. Blanch cucumbers for 5 minutes, then sauté in butter. Season with salt and white pepper.

PELICAN RESTAURANT
Clearwater Beach, Florida • illustration by Robert Curran Smith

A whimsical piece of driftwood shaped like a pelican is the center of attention in this popular eating place on the Gulf of Mexico owned by Henry Henriquez. The restaurant is open daily except Monday and serves continuously from 11:30 a.m. to 10:30 p.m. It is located at 470 Mandalay Avenue, Clearwater Beach, Florida.

Bread Custard Pudding

2½ cups milk	¼ teaspoon salt
4 eggs	1 cup bread crumbs
¾ cup sugar	¼ teaspoon nutmeg
1 teaspoon vanilla	

Heat milk. Beat eggs, add sugar, salt and vanilla. Slowly add milk to egg mixture, beating all of the time. Cover bottom of 9 x 5 x 3-inch pan with bread crumbs, pour custard over crumbs, sprinkle with nutmeg. Place pudding pan in a larger pan of water and bake at 350° for 35 to 40 minutes until set.

Thousand Island Dressing

Mix thoroughly: 2 cups mayonnaise; ½ cup ketchup; ½ cup chopped, cooked beets; ½ cup dill relish; ½ cup onion, chopped fine; and ½ green pepper, chopped fine. After mixing, place in jar and refrigerate. Makes about 1 quart of dressing.

SHERATON AT SANDESTIN
Destin, Florida • illustration by Miles Batt

Whether it's good food, comfortable rooms, golf, tennis, swimming, deep-sea fishing or just a plain relaxing vacation, you'll find it all at this 440-acre recreation reserve overlooking the Gulf of Mexico in north Florida. Located on U.S. Highway 98 about midway between Panama City and Pensacola, 8 miles east of the world-famous fishing capital of Destin. The accommodations include individual villas as well as 96 spacious rooms. Restaurant facilities range from informal grill rooms to the gourmet menu in the elegant Bay Club dining room. Golf and tennis packages are available.

Eggplant Antipasto

3 cups peeled and cubed eggplant	1 cup tomato paste
1/3 cup chopped green pepper	2 tablespoons wine vinegar
1 medium onion, coarsely chopped	1/2 cup green olives
3/4 cup sliced fresh mushrooms	1 1/2 teaspoons sugar
2 garlic cloves, chopped	1 teaspoon oregano
1/3 cup olive oil	1 teaspoon salt
	1 teaspoon pepper
	1/4 cup water

Put eggplant, green pepper, onion, mushrooms, garlic and oil in skillet. Cover and cook gently 10 minutes, stirring occasionally. Add tomato paste, vinegar, olives, sugar, oregano, salt, pepper and water. Mix well, cover and simmer until eggplant is tender, about 30 minutes. Serve hot or cold as appetizer.

LE CAFE DE PARIS

Fort Lauderdale, Florida • illustration by Walter Brightwell

There are six cozy dining rooms, each with a different atmosphere, at this famed French restaurant at 715 East Las Olas Boulevard. From I-95, take the E. Broward Exit. Louis Flematti and his family own and operate this establishment, which is open for lunch and dinner daily (dinner only on Sunday). Reservations necessary.

Lobster Café de Paris

2 2-pound lobsters	1/4 pound butter
1/3 cup chopped dry shallots	3 tablespoons flour
1 cup fresh sliced mushrooms	1/2 cup dry white wine
	3 cups light cream

2 tablespoons French mustard	1 1/2 cups grated Swiss cheese

Cook lobsters in court bouillon or seasoned water. Split them in halves. Remove meat from shells and cut in bite-size slices. Sauté mushrooms and shallots in butter. Add flour and cook 2-3 minutes. Gradually add wine, cream and mustard, stirring constantly. Simmer 8-10 minutes until sauce is medium thick. Fill bottom of shells with sauce, add meat and cover with remainder of sauce. Spread grated cheese over lobsters. Bake in 400° oven until cheese becomes golden brown. Serves 4.

MANERO'S RESTAURANT

Hallandale, Florida • illustration by Neil Boyle

Beef is king at this steak house, which has a dozen variations of fine prime meat on its menu. James Tiernan, the owner, is also justly proud of his famed Gorgonzola Salad. Lunch and dinner served weekdays; dinner only on Saturday and Sunday. It is at 2600 Hallandale Beach Boulevard, adjacent to the Inland Waterway Bridge, and just south of Hollywood.

Manero's Gorgonzola Salad

Mix 1 cup Mazola oil with 2 cloves of garlic in a blender. Rub salad bowl thoroughly with this mixture. Store leftover in a covered jar in the refrigerator. Break a head of lettuce into bite size pieces. Dice a green pepper, 2 stalks of celery and half an onion and add to lettuce in bowl. Chop 2 ripe tomatoes and place in bowl. Season to taste with salt and freshly ground pepper. Grate a 4-ounce piece of Gorgonzola cheese that has been chilled in the freezer for easier grating. Sprinkle grated cheese over salad. Combine ¼ cup cider vinegar with ¾ cup of Mazola oil. Pour enough to cover salad, toss and serve. Makes 4 portions.

PIGEON HOUSE PATIO
Key West, Florida • illustration by Ed Walaitis

The atmosphere here is relaxed and easy-paced, whether one is dining on the outdoor patio or on the veranda lined with hanging plants and vines. It is owned and operated by the Willard family, along with other restaurants in Key West. Open for lunch and dinner every day; reservations advisable. The address is 301-303 Whitehead Street, two blocks from Mile Marker 0 on U.S. Highway 1.

Shrimp Cayo Hueso

Shell 4 pounds medium-size raw shrimp. Wrap each shrimp in a slice of thinly sliced bacon (about 1 pound). Broil shrimp on both sides until bacon is cooked. Serve over Bahamian rice and top with cheese sauce (below). Serves 8-10.

Bahamian Rice

3 tablespoons oil	1 tablespoon salt
1 cup chopped onion	1 teaspoon pepper
½ cup tomato paste	4½ cups water
1 tablespoon leaf thyme	2 cups rice

Heat oil, add onion and sauté until tender. Stir in tomato paste, thyme, salt, pepper and water. Bring to boiling, stir in rice, cover and simmer over low heat about 20 minutes or until all liquid is absorbed. Let stand, covered, about 1 hour.

Cheese Sauce

6 tablespoons butter	½ tablespoon sweet
6 tablespoons flour	basil
2 13-ounce cans	1 teaspoon salt
evaporated milk	1 teaspoon pepper
3 cups chicken stock	2 tablespoons
½ teaspoon ground	Worcestershire sauce
cardamom	1 pound Cheddar
	cheese, shredded

Melt butter in large saucepan. Stir in flour and blend well. Slowly stir in milk, then chicken broth and cook and stir until sauce is smooth and slightly thickened. Add cardamom, sweet basil, salt, pepper and Worcestershire. Reduce heat, gradually add cheese and stir until smooth.

THE FORGE
Miami Beach, Florida • illustration by Alexander Kortner

This fine restaurant is housed in a French Empire townhouse at 432 Arthur Godfrey Road. Owner Alvin Malnik has designed the dining rooms around his collection of old stained glass. His bronzes, jades, ivories, paintings and antique furnishings give diners the impression that they are enjoying dinner in an elegant private home. Dinner only — reservations necessary. From Collins Avenue turn on 41st Street. The Forge is three blocks on the left.

Crepes Hongroises

Make 25 six-inch crepes, stack crepes on a platter. Make a filling by combining 2 cups ground walnuts, ⅓ cup whipping cream, ½ cup apricot preserves and 2 tablespoons rum. Spread 1 teaspoon of apricot mixture on each crepe. Roll crepes cigar-fashion, place in well buttered baking dish and bake 10 minutes in a 350° oven. Serve with a sprinkling of powdered sugar and a dab of apricot preserve on each crepe.

Creamed Spinach

3 pounds fresh spinach	½ cup heavy cream
1½ cups thick Béchamel sauce (below)	1 garlic clove, finely chopped
¾ cup mayonnaise	Grated nutmeg, salt and pepper to taste.

Wash and drain spinach. Steam in water left from washing just until tender. Drain and chop fine. Blend into Béchamel sauce with mayonnaise, cream, garlic and seasonings. Stir well and reheat quickly just before serving. Serves 6.

Béchamel Sauce

Melt 3 tablespoons butter and stir in 3 tablespoons flour with wooden spoon. Cook and stir until mixture is bubbly. Add 1½ cups milk, stirring constantly. Bring to boiling, then cook 3 minutes on low heat until sauce thickens. Season to taste with salt and white pepper.

Poulet Lausannier

2 frying chickens, cut in serving pieces	2 finely chopped onions
¼ teaspoon dried thyme	Tomato Sauce (below)
Salt and pepper to taste	½ pound fresh mushrooms, sliced
3 tablespoons butter	Chopped fresh parsley
3 tablespoons vegetable oil	White rice ring
4 garlic cloves, crushed	

Sprinkle chicken with thyme, salt and pepper. In large skillet heat butter and oil over medium heat. Add chicken pieces and brown on both sides. Add crushed garlic and cook about 3 minutes more. Remove chicken from skillet and place in buttered

baking pan. In the same skillet, sauté onions until just golden brown and set aside. Add mushrooms to Tomato Sauce and spread over chicken. Cover baking dish with aluminum foil and bake in 350° oven 45 minutes to 1 hour. Serve sprinkled with chopped fresh parsley in rice ring. Serves 7 to 8.

Tomato Sauce

1 6-ounce can tomato paste	1-2 tablespoons sugar, or more to taste
½ cup dry sherry	1 teaspoon mild prepared mustard
Salt and pepper to taste	
⅛ teaspoon dried basil	1 cup well-drained chopped canned tomatoes
1-2 tablespoons wine vinegar, or more to taste	

In mixing bowl blend well tomato paste, sherry, salt, pepper, basil, vinegar, sugar and mustard. Add tomato mixture to onions in skillet in which chicken was browned and simmer about 4 minutes, stirring constantly. Add chopped tomatoes and cook, stirring constantly, until a smooth paste is formed.

Shrimp Merlin

In a large sauce pan bring 3 quarts of water to boil, add 1 tablespoon powdered thyme and ½ teaspoon basil. When water boils, add 2 pounds large, shelled and deveined raw shrimp (do not defrost if frozen). Bring to a boil again, reduce heat and simmer for approximately 5 minutes or until shrimp are pink and tender. Drain and cool completely. In a large bowl combine 1 quart jar of mayonnaise, a 4-ounce jar of capers and juice, 2 medium onions, sliced in thin slices, 1 teaspoon dry mustard and ¼ teaspoon coarsely ground black pepper. Add cooled shrimp and mix well. Refrigerate for 24 hours before serving on beds of lettuce. Serves 6.

Forge Strawberry Shortcake

For individual servings use 6 brandy snifters or glass bowls. Place one slice of pound cake in the bottom of each dish and sprinkle each piece with brandy or Cointreau. Let stand. In the meantime toss together 3 cups sliced strawberries, 1½ cups sugar and 1 teaspoon vanilla. Place a generous layer of the strawberry mixture over the cake slices, cover with a second slice of pound cake and sprinkle with liqueur. Place another layer of berries over cake. Use a pastry bag to cover the cake slices with 3 cups sweetened whipped cream. Garnish with remaining berries and top each with a whole strawberry. Serves 6.

COLONY BEACH AND TENNIS RESORT
Sarasota, Florida

One of the finest dining and entertainment complexes in the area, this resort is located at 1620 Gulf of Mexico Drive on Longboat Key. International cuisine is featured and the club is particularly famous for its English Hunt Brunch on Sundays from 11:30 a.m. to 2:30 p.m. Breakfast, lunch and dinner served daily. Reservations advisable.

Louisiana Pepper Steak

2 pounds beef tenderloin slices, cut in thin strips	½ teaspoon chopped fresh garlic
3 tablespoons olive oil	2 bay leaves
4 green peppers, diced	1 tablespoon Maggi sauce
1 large Spanish onion, diced	1 tablespoon Ac'cent
2 pimentos, diced	1 cup beef broth
	2 tablespoons flour

Sauté beef strips in hot oil until browned. Add green peppers, onion, pimentos, garlic; cook and stir almost constantly until vegetables are tender. Add bay leaves, Maggi and Ac'cent. Blend beef broth with flour, stir in and bring to boiling, stirring until thickened. Remove bay leaves and serve over rice or noodles. Serves 4 to 6.

ANTHONY'S
Atlanta, Georgia • illustration by Robert W. Bragg

Housed in an authentically restored 1797 plantation home, Anthony's is tucked away in a wooded area at 3109 Piedmont Road, N.E. Enjoy its antebellum cuisine with a French accent in the open-hearth kitchen or the elegant crystal-chandeliered parlors. Open every day except Sunday 6 p.m. to 11 p.m.

Chocolate Pecan Pie

2 ounces unsweetened chocolate	Dash salt
2 tablespoons butter	3 eggs
½ cup corn syrup	½ cup bourbon
1 cup sugar	1 cup pecans, chopped
	Unbaked 9-inch pie shell

Melt chocolate and butter in top of double boiler. Combine corn syrup and sugar in saucepan and simmer 2 minutes. Add chocolate mixture and cool slightly. Add salt to eggs and beat slightly. Slowly dribble syrup mixture into eggs, stirring constantly. Blend in bourbon and nuts. Spoon into pie shell and bake in preheated 325° oven 30 minutes. Cool and serve with whipped cream.

GOETCHIUS HOUSE
Columbus, Georgia • illustration by Frederick Carter

Shaded by giant oaks, sugarberry and pecan trees, the charming old home is in the historic section of the city. Open daily for lunch and dinner; closed

Sunday and some holidays. Reservations recommended.

Country Captain

4-pound tender chicken, or equal weight of chicken breasts
Seasoned flour
3 tablespoons lard
2 onions, finely chopped
2 green peppers, chopped
1 small garlic clove, minced
1½ teaspoons salt
½ teaspoon white pepper
3 teaspoons curry powder

2 No. 2 cans of stewed tomatoes
½ teaspoon chopped parsley
½ teaspoon powdered thyme
3 heaping tablespoons currants
¼ pound slivered, toasted almonds
2 cups cooked rice
Parsley for garnish

Disjoint chicken, remove skin and roll pieces in flour seasoned with salt, pepper. Brown in lard. Remove chicken from pan, but keep it hot. Put onions, peppers and garlic into the pan. Cook very slowly, stirring constantly. Season with salt, pepper and curry powder. Add tomatoes, parsley, thyme. Put chicken in roaster and pour mixture over it. If it does not cover chicken, rinse pan with water and pour this over chicken. Cover roaster tightly. Bake in moderate oven for 45 minutes or until chicken is tender. Place chicken in the center of a platter, surround with rice. Drop currants into sauce; pour over rice. Scatter almonds on top. Garnish with parsley. Serves 8.

NEW PERRY HOTEL
Perry, Georgia • illustration by Robert W. Bragg

This gracious hostelry has been owned for 33 years by Mr. and Mrs. J. Yates Green and Harold F. Green.

The dining room and coffee shop are justly famous for their many Southern specialties. The address is 800 Main Street. From I-75 take U.S. 341 to the center of town. Breakfast, lunch and dinner served every day. Overnight accommodations in the hotel and motel; reservations advisable.

Shredded Yams

Mix 1 cup sugar, ½ cup white Karo syrup and ½ cup water. Cook until mixture becomes a simple syrup. Add ½ stick margarine or butter. Shred 2 pounds of raw sweet potatoes (yams) in a gallon of water, using a shredded salad maker with No. 5 cone. Add 1 tablespoon salt. Drain and wash well. Pour shredded yams in any shallow pan. Pour 1 cup pineapple juice (or orange juice) over yams, then pour in syrup. Bake in 350° oven for 35 minutes or until yams are transparent. Serves 12.

Lemon Chess Pie

½ cup butter
1½ cups sugar
1 tablespoon cornstarch
4 eggs

Juice and rind of 2 lemons
9-inch unbaked pie shell

Cream butter. Blend sugar and cornstarch together, add to creamed butter and blend well. Add eggs one at a time, beat well after each is added. Stir in lemon juice and grated rinds. Pour into pie shell and bake in 350° oven for 35 minutes.

PLANTATION ROOM
Pine Mountain, Georgia • illustration by Robert W. Bragg

Southern and Continental cooking are the specialties at the fine dining room in the Gardens Holiday Inn, just a stone's throw from the beautiful all-season Callaway Gardens. Breakfast, lunch and dinner served every day. It is on U.S. 27 in Pine Mountain in western Georgia. Overnight accommodations and complete vacation facilities available; reservations advisable.

Strawberries Romanoff

1 quart of fresh strawberries	2 tablespoons melba sauce
4 ounces Grand Marnier	3 cups lightly sweetened whipped cream
4 tablespoons sugar	
Rind of 2 oranges, grated	4 scoops soft vanilla ice cream

Wash strawberries and remove stems and place in a bowl. Add Grand Marnier, sugar, orange rind and melba sauce. Toss a few times to blend. Cover and chill for 1 hour. Remove berries from refrigerator, add whipped cream and mix. Add ice cream and stir until well blended. Divide into sherbet glasses or a single deep dessert dish. Serves 6.

Callaway Carrot Soufflé

1 pound carrots (about 5), cooked	1 teaspoon baking powder
4 large eggs	1 teaspoon nutmeg
½ cup sugar	1 pinch salt and allspice
¾ cup flour	1 tablespoon butter, melted

Beat carrots in mixer. Add eggs one at a time, beating well. Sift dry ingredients and blend into carrot mixture. Add butter. Bake in 6-cup buttered pan for 30 minutes at 350° or until puffed and firm. Serves 4.

BLANCHE'S COURTYARD
St. Simons Island, Georgia • illustration by Betty Lowe

This charming restaurant features coastal seafood cooking in a relaxed friendly atmosphere. Lunch served in season; evening dining the year round. Dixie Band music each weekend; closed Sunday. From U.S. 17 take Torras Causeway to the Village-Fishing Pier section of St. Simons. Blanche's is in the heart of the Old Village. Pat and Rip Benton are the owners.

Old South Bread Pudding

3 cups milk	½ teaspoon nutmeg
2 tablespoons butter	½ teaspoon cinnamon
3 eggs	1 cup raisins
½ cup sugar	7 slices day-old bread
½ teaspoon salt	

Scald milk and butter together. Beat eggs and sugar together, then add salt and spices, raisins and scalded milk mixture. Shred bread and place in a buttered baking dish; pour mixture over bread and bake in 350° oven for about 45 minutes. To keep mixture from sticking, baking dish may be placed in a pan of water while in the oven. Serve with sauce (below).

Pudding Sauce

Cream together ¼ pound butter with ¾ cup sugar. Then add 3 tablespoons warm milk or cream and 3-4 tablespoons whiskey. Serve hot over warm or cold bread pudding. Makes 6 portions.

DESOTO HILTON HOTEL
Savannah, Georgia • illustration by Richard Mantia

The formal dining room — the Pavilion — is famous for its fine wine list and Continental cuisine. Lunch and dinner served daily; reservations advisable. The hotel, at Bull and Liberty Streets, is in downtown Savannah. Take the Downtown Exit from I-16 onto Liberty Street. Overnight accommodations and recreation facilities at the hotel. Ted Kleisner is the manager.

Sea Trout Wellington

2 to 2½ pounds sea trout filets	Salmon Mousse filling (below), prepared in advance
⅓ cup white wine	
1 tablespoon butter	Egg wash (1 egg yolk beaten with 2 tablespoons water)
Salt and white pepper	
Quick puff pastry (below)	

Place filets on baking pan, sprinkle with wine, butter, salt and pepper. Bake at 400° about 15 minutes or until fish flakes. Cool. Roll pastry ⅛-inch thick. Line 3½-cup-capacity tin-lined fish mold with pastry and trim off excess around edges. Line the pastry with parchment paper and fill with uncooked rice. (This will reduce shrinkage and improve impression of mold on finished pastry.) Cut separate piece of pastry to fit mold to serve as cover crust. Bake at 350° for 20 minutes, remove from oven and remove parchment paper and rice filling. Return to oven and bake additional 15 minutes. Remove cover crust when lightly browned, and set aside.

After mold has been baked and cooled, remove pastry shell and fill with fish and mousse in the following manner: Line the shell with 1 trout filet, then add mousse and level. Cover the mousse with the second filet and cover with the pre-baked pastry crust. Invert full shell on greased baking sheet and brush with egg wash. Return to oven and bake at 350° for 10 minutes, or to a microwave for 2 minutes. (Use parchment paper instead of baking pan in microwave.) Place on silver platter, garnish with lemon stars, parsley and vegetable accompaniments. Serve with hollandaise sauce. Serves 2 to 3.

Quick Puff Pastry

1⅓ cups sifted all-purpose flour	⅔ cup vegetable shortening
½ teaspoon salt	½ cup ice water
½ cup butter	

On a cold board or marble slab, sift flour and salt together. Make a well in center, add butter, shortening and half the water. Work together and gather into a ball. Add more water if needed. Chill work surface with ice cubes, wipe dry, then dust with flour and roll dough into rectangular shape. Fold pastry, top to center, bottom to center, bottom to top, then turn clockwise and roll out. Repeat this same folding procedure 4 times. Wrap in plastic and store in refrigerator 24 hours.

Salmon Mousse Filling

1 pound fresh salmon	½ teaspoon cayenne pepper
3 egg whites	
1 cup heavy cream	½ teaspoon dry mustard
½ cup sour cream	½ cup chopped pistachio nuts
1 teaspoon salt	
1½ teaspoons nutmeg	

Pound salmon in a mortar until smooth. Add egg whites to salmon in mixing bowl immersed in ice. Beat 5 minutes. Add cream in slow steady stream while continuing to mix an additional 8 minutes. Mix in sour cream, salt, nutmeg, pepper, mustard and nuts until mixture is smooth. Pour into buttered mold and steam for 12 minutes. Remove and let stand until cool.

JOHNNY HARRIS RESTAURANT
Savannah, Georgia • illustration by Robert W. Bragg

In 1924 the Johnny Harris family started this restaurant as a barbecue stand which was later expanded into a large and friendly restaurant now owned by the Donaldson family. Open for lunch and dinner every weekday; closed Sunday. The address is 1651 East Victory Drive about 10 minutes from town.

Johnny Harris Onion Soup

6 medium onions, sliced thin	7 cups boiling water
1 stick butter or margarine, melted	½ cup sherry
	Salt
1 teaspoon sugar	Big croutons
3 shakes ground nutmeg	Grated Parmesan cheese
8 rounded teaspoons beef stock base	

Sauté sliced onions in melted butter with sugar and nutmeg. Cook until onions are transparent, but not browned. Dissolve beef stock base in boiling water in a large saucepan. Add onions and simmer for about 20 minutes. Add sherry during the last 2 minutes of cooking. Taste, and add salt if needed. Spoon into serving dishes; add croutons and top with grated Parmesan. Broil for about 10 minutes. Serves 6-8.

THE PIRATES' HOUSE

Savannah, Georgia • illustration by William E. Pauli

Located on the site of Georgia's Trustees' Garden, this family-oriented restaurant is actually eight ancient buildings which have been joined together. One of them, the Herb House, built in 1734, is the state's oldest standing structure. A rendezvous spot for pirates in the late 1700s, and the setting for part of Robert Louis Stevenson's classic *Treasure Island*, the Pirates' House is Savannah's most famous restaurant. Located one short block from the Savannah River, the restaurant serves meals from 11:30 a.m. to 10:45 p.m. daily. Closed Christmas day. Owner and host Herb Traub encourages diners to browse through the 23 dining rooms before sampling the superb Southern cuisine.

Miss Edna's Seafood Bisque

1 10-ounce can condensed green pea soup	*3 cups milk*
	½ pound crab meat
	½ pound boiled shrimp
1 10-ounce can condensed tomato soup	*½ cup sherry*

Blend soups with milk. Heat and add crab meat, shrimp and sherry just before serving. Add a twist of lemon peel to each bowl of soup. Serves 6.

Pirates' House Trifle

1 pint whipping cream	*1 pound angel food cake*
¾ cup sherry	
1 quart boiled egg custard	

Whip cream and sweeten to taste. Add ¼ cup sherry. Add balance of sherry to egg custard. Cut cake into thin layers. Use 2-quart casserole. Place layer of cake in bottom; add custard and then whipped cream.

Alternate layers ending with whipped cream on top. Let set in refrigerator for at least one hour before serving. Serves 8.

Savannah Red Rice

¼ pound bacon	*½ teaspoon salt*
½ cup chopped onions	*¼ teaspoon pepper*
2 cups raw rice	*⅛ teaspoon Tabasco*
2 cups tomatoes	

Fry bacon until crisp. Remove from pan. Cook the onions tender in bacon fat. Add washed rice, tomatoes, seasonings and crumbled bacon. Cook over low heat about 10 minutes. Pour into 1-quart casserole. Cover tightly. Bake at 350° for one hour, stirring with fork several times. Serves 6 to 8.

THE BRASS LANTERN

Aurora, Kentucky • illustration by Ken Holland

An old homestead was remodeled to achieve an air of rustic elegance. It is less than a mile from the shores of Kentucky Lake and the Land Between the Lakes on U.S. 68, between State Highways 80 and 94, in the western part of the state. Open for dinner every day, except Monday and Tuesday. Closed December 21 to March 25. Carol and Dick Thomas are the owner-chefs.

Grasshopper Pie

Melt together in the top of a double boiler 24 large marshmallows in ½ cup of milk. Cool. Add 1 ounce white crème de cacao and 1 ounce green crème de menthe, then fold in ½ pint of whipping cream, whipped. Pour into chilled 9-inch chocolate wafer pie shell. Chill in freezer until ready to serve.

Steak Sauterne

Cut 1½ pounds of filet mignon into bite-sized pieces. Sauté 1 large green pepper, cut into strips, with 6 sliced mushroom caps in 2 tablespoons butter until tender. Add ½ cup tomato sauce, ¼ teaspoon each of oregano and garlic salt. Cook steak pieces medium on a charcoal grill or oven broiler. Season with salt and pepper while cooking. Add cooked meat to tomato sauce. Add ½ cup sauterne wine. Heat mixture when ready to serve. Serve over 2 cups hot rice. Makes 4 portions.

BOONE TAVERN HOTEL
Berea, Kentucky • illustration by Louis Peck

This lovely old Georgian hotel is located in the center of the beautiful Berea College campus and is staffed by students. Breakfast, lunch and dinner served daily. Reservations advisable for meals and overnight accommodations. Take Berea exit from I-75, turn left and go one mile to Berea College.

Southern Peanut Soup

1 cup finely chopped cooked ham	2 cups finely cut green onions (1 cup onion and 1 cup green tops)
2 cups unsalted peanuts, blanched and chopped fine (blanched salted peanuts can be washed in hot water to remove salt)	½ cup butter or margarine
	1 cup sifted flour
	1½ quarts chicken stock
	1 quart beef stock

Sauté ham, peanuts and white onion in butter. Add flour, blending and cooking about 4 minutes. Stir constantly to prevent sticking. Add the soup stocks and blend with a wire whip and cook for 15 minutes. Stir occasionally. Just before serving, add the onion tops and simmer 10 minutes. Yields 16 servings. (From Richard J. Hougen's cookbook — *More Hougen Favorites* ®1971.)

Kentucky Blackberry Dumplings

1 15-ounce can blackberries	1 teaspoon lemon juice
½ cup sugar	Pastry for 2 9-inch crusts
2 tablespoons cornstarch	Milk Dip (below)
Pinch salt	
1 tablespoon butter	

Drain blackberries and place juice in top of double boiler. Mix in sugar, cornstarch and salt. Cook stirring, until thickened. Remove from heat, stir in butter, lemon juice and blackberries and set aside. Roll out pastry and cut each into 4 wedges. Place a generous tablespoon of berry mixture in the center of each pie crust wedge and bring edges together, pinch to close the dumpling. Place on baking sheet and bake at 450° for 15 minutes. Serve warm with Milk Dip. Makes 8 portions.

Milk Dip

3 cups milk	6 tablespoons butter
¾ cup sugar	1½ teaspoons vanilla
2½ tablespoons cornstarch	

Heat the milk in top of double boiler. Mix sugar and cornstarch and stir into milk. Cook and stir until smooth and thickened. Stir in butter and vanilla and serve hot over dumplings.

DANNY'S
Baltimore, Maryland • illustration by John Vanides

Located on Charles Street at Biddle, in the heart of Baltimore, Danny's features Chesapeake Bay seafood and Continental specialties. Lunch and dinner served

Monday through Friday; on Saturday, only dinner. Closed Sunday.

Caesar Salad

Cut a clove of garlic and rub salad bowl thoroughly. Add 6 ounces cleaned inside leaves of romaine lettuce. Pour 3 ounces garlic olive oil over lettuce. Add ½ teaspoon Worcestershire sauce, dash of freshly ground pepper and salt. Add 1 coddled egg and toss lettuce lightly. Pour juice of 1 lemon over salad and toss again. Add 2 ounces croutons, 2 ounces Parmesan cheese and toss salad again. Cut 4 large flat Spanish anchovies into bite-size pieces and add to salad. Toss and serve. Makes 2 portions.

Fruit de Mer en Coquille

2 ounces butter	Salt and white pepper,
2 teaspoons chopped	to taste
shallots	Pinch of cayenne
¼ cup sliced mushrooms	½ cup Mornay sauce
2 ounces lump crab	½ cup whipping cream,
2 ounces lobster meat	whipped
2 ounces scallops	2 tablespoons
¼ cup Chablis	hollandaise sauce

Sauté shallots in melted butter. Add mushrooms, seafood and wine. Cook gently until wine is reduced to half. Season and stir in Mornay sauce. Add whipped cream and mix again. Pour into shell-shaped oven dish. Top with hollandaise. Brown under broiler. Serves 2.

PIMLICO HOTEL RESTAURANT
Baltimore, Maryland • illustration by Tom Green

Generous servings of expertly prepared food at reasonable prices add up to the great popularity of this restaurant. The enormous menu of seafoods, steaks, Chinese specialties and homemade desserts is a plus. Formerly a hotel, the building has been converted into a series of dining rooms. A nearby attraction is the Pimlico Race Track. Reservations necessary for lunch and dinner served daily. Late night snacks are popular. The address is 5301 Park Heights Avenue near Baltimore Beltway 695.

Filet of Flounder Audrey

6 filets of flounder (10 to 12 ounces each)	9 tablespoons green or natural pistachios
Salt and pepper	1 tablespoon lemon
½ cup flour	juice
½ cup clarified butter	1½ cups white wine
3 tablespoons chopped shallots	

Sprinkle filets with salt and pepper; dredge lightly with flour. Heat butter in large skillet. Add fish and brown lightly on both sides. Add shallots and pistachios. Cook ½ minute. Add lemon juice and wine. Cook 2 minutes. Remove filets to hot serving platter. Quickly cook sauce to reduce about half. Pour over fish and garnish with watercress. Serves 6.

OLD SOUTH MOUNTAIN INN
Boonsboro, Maryland • illustration by Harvey Kidder

This historic inn on U.S. Alternate Route 40, east of Boonsboro, has welcomed travelers for nearly 250 years. It stands beside the Appalachian Trail and Washington Monument State Park, 50 miles from Washington, D.C., and Baltimore, Maryland. Lunch and dinner served every day, except Monday.

Fluffy Frozen Peanut Butter Pie

½ cup cream cheese
1⅓ cups confectioners'
  sugar
7½ tablespoons peanut
  butter
½ cup milk
1⅛ cups non-dairy
  whipped topping

8-inch graham cracker
  pie shell, baked and
  cooled
¼ cup finely chopped
  peanuts

Whip cheese at low speed until soft and fluffy. Beat in sugar and peanut butter at medium speed. Slowly beat in milk. Fold topping into mixture. Pour into pie shell and sprinkle with chopped nuts. Freeze until firm and then serve cut into wedges. If stored for any length of time, wrap pie when frozen hard.

THE TIDEWATER INN

Easton, Maryland • illustration by Bruce Bond

Noted for its Southern hospitality and its charm, this Eastern Shore hostelry has complete vacation facilities. Breakfast, lunch and dinner are served daily; reservations necessary for meals and overnight accommodations. It is about 75 miles east of Washington, D.C. From U.S. 50 turn right on Dover Street and proceed a half mile to Harrison Street in the center of Easton. The restaurant is on the corner of Dover and Harrison Streets. Anton J. Hoevenaars is the manager.

Crab Imperial

Mix together 4 tablespoons mayonnaise, ¾ teaspoon Worcestershire sauce, ¼ teaspoon salt, dash of Tabasco and a pinch each of thyme, oregano, dry mustard and Accent. Mix well and stir in an egg, then blend well with 1 pound crab meat. Coat a casserole lightly with mayonnaise and fill with crab mixture.

Spread a thin layer of mayonnaise over the top and sprinkle with paprika and parsley. Bake at 350° for 35-45 minutes. Serves 4.

Escalloped Oysters

1 quart oysters
3 cups crushed saltine
  crackers
Salt and pepper, to taste
1 teaspoon chicken
  bouillon (granulated)

2 tablespoons melted
  butter
2 cups milk, or enough
  to cover
Parsley and paprika

Mix crushed crackers with salt, pepper and bouillon. In a casserole make alternate layers of cracker mixture and oysters, making the last layer of crackers. Combine melted butter with enough milk to cover casserole. Sprinkle with parsley and paprika. Bake at 325° for 35 minutes. Serves 4-6.

A RESTAURANT BY GEORGE

Nags Head, North Carolina • illustration by Fred Browning

Near Jockey Ridge State Park and Wright Brothers National Museum, this informal restaurant is about an hour's drive from Cape Hatteras. Diners can watch their food orders being prepared in the kitchen through a large glass-paneled wall. Dinner served every day. Closed the day after Thanksgiving until the first of March. It is near Milepost 11½ on the business section of U.S. Highway 158 in Nags Head.

Bottoms-Up

24 large fresh
  mushrooms
1 pound well-picked
  lump crab meat
¼ large green pepper
¼ medium onion

⅓ cup sour cream
⅓ cup mayonnaise
1 tablespoon prepared
  mustard
Salt and pepper, to taste

Place picked crab in a mixing bowl. Add finely minced onions and green peppers to crab meat along with other ingredients except mushrooms. Be careful when folding ingredients together to preserve lump texture of crab. Wash mushrooms and remove stems. Stuff caps with crab mixture and place in refrigerator for at least 2 hours. Bake in 350° oven until mushrooms are tender, about 10 minutes. Brown off under broiler and serve immediately. Makes 6 portions.

PINEHURST HOTEL
Pinehurst, North Carolina • illustration by Richard A. Young

For over 80 years this has been one of America's most famous resort hotels. There are championship golf courses, tennis courts, and horseback riding paths on the extensive landscaped grounds. Breakfast, lunch and dinner served; overnight accommodations. The executive chef, Sture Andersson, is one of eight chefs selected for the 1976 U.S. team in the Culinary Olympics. Take Pinehurst exit from U.S. Highway 1. Joseph M. Grantham, Jr., is Director of Resort Operations and general manager.

Chocolate Fondue

6 ounces unsweetened chocolate	*Bite size pieces of sponge cake, and*
1¾ cups sugar	*fresh or canned fruits*
1 cup light cream	*at room temperature*
½ cup butter	*(bananas, oranges,*
4 tablespoons Curaçao	*apples, pears, etc.)*
2 tablespoons grated orange rind	

Melt chocolate in double broiler or over low heat. Add sugar, cream and butter, and mix thoroughly. Add liqueur and rind. Pour into fondue pot or casserole dish and keep warm. Use fondue forks, toothpicks or shrimp forks to spear cake and fruit and dip in chocolate. Serves 6. (Use stainless steel knife when cutting citrus fruits, otherwise fruits discolor. Dip fruits such as bananas, apples and pears in water mixed with lemon juice to keep from discoloring.)

Chicken Breast Charlotte Amelie

Sprinkle 4 large chicken breasts with salt and dip in flour. Sauté in ½ cup vegetable oil until done and remove chicken from pan. To the oil in which chicken was cooked, add ½ cup finely chopped onions and 1½ teaspoons finely chopped garlic. Sauté until soft. Reduce heat and add 1 teaspoon *each* of turmeric, ground cumin, ground hot red pepper and ground coriander. Add 1 mashed banana and ½ cup whipping cream. If necessary to thicken sauce, add a little cornstarch mixed with water. Cut 4 whole coconuts in halves lengthwise and pour milk into onion mixture and stir well. Cut out some of the meat from the coconut and grate. Then lightly toast the coconut and keep in reserve. Place one chicken breast in 4 of the coconut halves. Spoon on sauce; if any is left, serve separately. Put other coconut half on and seal cut with a ½-inch-wide strip of pie dough. Brush dough with beaten egg yolk. Bake in 375° oven. This will reheat chicken by the time the dough is baked. Break away dough and lift off cover. Place each coconut in middle of rice ring made from plain steamed rice. Sprinkle with toasted coconut. Serve with broiled bananas, kumquats, toasted coconut, almonds or raisins.

DARRYL'S 1849 RESTAURANT
Raleigh, North Carolina • illustration by Miles Batt

Located at 6008 Glenwood Avenue (the Raleigh-Durham Highway), this is a multilevel restaurant, in the decor of the 1849 gold rush days. Lunch and dinner served every day. Reservations not necessary.

Lasagna

1 pound ground beef
¼ pound mild Italian sausage, peeled
½ teaspoon granulated garlic
6 cups tomato sauce
12 ounces tomato paste
1 tablespoon oregano
1 teaspoon crushed rosemary
3 teaspoons salt
1½ teaspoons black pepper
½ cup dry red wine
1 pound lasagna noodles, uncooked
2 eggs
2 pounds creamed cottage cheese, small curd
1 pound Mozzarella cheese, sliced

In a large frying pan, mix ground beef, sausage and garlic. Brown slowly until all of the fat is cooked off. Drain excess fat. To the drained meat add tomato sauce, tomato paste, oregano, rosemary, 2 teaspoons salt, ½ teaspoon pepper and wine. Mix well and simmer over low heat for 30 minutes, stirring often. Prepare lasagna noodles according to package instructions. Beat together eggs, remaining salt and pepper and then mix with cottage cheese. Lightly grease a 13x9x2-inch casserole. Layer half of noodles, half of cottage cheese mixture and half of cheese and half of meat sauce, then repeat. Cover and bake in 350° oven for about 45 minutes. Let cool 10 minutes. Serves 10-12.

THE SHAW HOUSE TEA ROOM
Southern Pines, North Carolina • illustration by Richard A. Young

Located at the southern entrance of Southern Pines, at the corner of S.W. Broad and Morganton Road, this charming old house is typical of the rustic cabins which housed the first settlers of the region. The Shaw House is open to visitors from February 1 to May 1 for luncheons and afternoon tea. The tea room proceeds are devoted to the upkeep of the house and grounds. Reservations advisable.

Shaw House Prune Cake

3 eggs beaten
1½ cups granulated sugar
1 cup cooking oil
2 cups flour
1 teaspoon baking soda
1 teaspoon salt
1 teaspoon cinnamon
½ teaspoon ground allspice
1 cup buttermilk
1 cup chopped cooked prunes

Add sugar and oil to beaten eggs. Sift flour with baking soda, salt and spices. Add buttermilk and flour mixture alternately to the batter. Stir in chopped prunes. Bake in 2 round 8- or 9-inch cake pans for 35 minutes in a 350° oven. Frost cooled layers with icing (below).

Buttercream Icing

Cream ¼ cup softened butter with 2 cups confectioners' sugar. Blend in 2 tablespoons cream and 1 teaspoon of vanilla.

MILLS HYATT HOUSE
Charleston, South Carolina • illustration by Al Satterwhite

This hotel is located in the heart of the historic section of Charleston which is considered one of the most beautiful cities in America. The 250-room hotel is on the site of the original Mills House Hotel which was completed in 1853. The Barbados Room, the main dining room, is open for breakfast, lunch and dinner. Reservations advisable for meals and for hotel accommodations. The hotel is at the corner of Meeting and Queen Streets.

Mills House Wilted Spinach Salad

½ pound well-washed
   spinach
½ cup well-seasoned
   vinaigrette dressing
1 hard-cooked egg,
   chopped
2 strips crisp cooked
   bacon, chopped
⅓ cup crumbled blue
   cheese

Wash and dry spinach. Remove stems, tear into bite-sized pieces and place in salad bowl. Pour vinaigrette dressing into hot skillet. Stir in egg, bacon and cheese and mix well. Pour onto spinach, toss and serve immediately.

ROBERT'S OF CHARLESTON

Charleston, South Carolina • illustration by Fred Browning

This unusual restaurant features fine foods and music, opera arias and pop medleys sung by the owner-chef, Robert Dickson. When the 28 guests (by reservation only) are seated at 8 p.m., no more are admitted and the dinner proceeds through quiche, salad, seafood, Chateaubriand, dessert and coffee with appropriate wines. Between courses the rich baritone of Robert fills this small restaurant. Open for dinner only Tuesday through Saturday, it is closed Easter, Thanksgiving and Christmas weeks and August. The fixed price of $27 includes wine and service. The address is 42 North Market Street close to I-26 and U.S. Highway 17.

Spinach Quiche

Pastry

4 cups flour
1 teaspoon salt
1¼ cups soft butter
2 eggs
½ cup cold water

Place flour, butter and salt in large bowl and work with pastry cutter until small lumps are formed. Add eggs with water, gather dough together in your hands and shape into a round. Refrigerate 4 hours or more. Roll out to fit 3 9-inch pie pans. Cover each with piece of foil, pressing down. Bake at 350° 15 to 20 minutes.

Batter

1 medium onion,
   chopped
½ cup olive oil
2 10-ounce packages
   frozen chopped
   spinach, thawed
2 to 3 garlic cloves,
   chopped
2 tablespoons chopped
   shallots
9 eggs
3 cups heavy cream
Grated nutmeg, salt,
   pepper
1 pound Swiss
   Emmenthaler cheese
Robert's Seasoning
   (optional — available
   at restaurant)
3 pre-baked pie shells

Sauté onion in oil in large skillet until soft. Squeeze all liquid from spinach and add to pan with garlic and shallots. Cook on medium heat 15 minutes. Cool. Lightly beat eggs and cream together. Grate or finely slice cheese, add to eggs, then stir in spinach mixture. Season to taste. Spoon into pre-baked pie shells, filling to just below top of crust. Bake in middle of 400° oven 30 to 40 minutes, until puffed and firm to touch. Let rest before cutting. Makes 3 pies.

Vinaigrette Dressing

In food processor or blender place 2 eggs, ½ cup tarragon vinegar, ½ teaspoon chopped garlic, 1 tablespoon chopped shallots, 1 teaspoon dried tarragon, 1 teaspoon sweet basil, 1½ teaspoons pepper, 1½ teaspoons salt. Blend 20 seconds. Slowly blend in 1 cup olive oil and 1 cup peanut oil until creamy consistency is formed.

THE GREENBRIAR

Florence, South Carolina • illustration by John Arvan

A charming turn-of-the-century residence was completely renovated and converted into this fine dining place at 255 South Irby Street (intersection of U.S. 301, 76 and 52) in the center of Florence. Lunch and dinner served Monday through Friday; dinner only on Saturday; closed Sunday. Reservations requested.

Creamed Broccoli

1 10-ounce package
   frozen chopped
   broccoli
1 cup sour cream
2 tablespoons lemon
   juice
¼ teaspoon crushed
   oregano leaves
¼ cup melted butter
¼ teaspoon salt

Cook broccoli according to package directions and season with salt and pepper. Drain. Add remaining ingredients, mix thoroughly and serve hot. Makes 4 generous servings.

Greenbriar Special Salad Dressing

Into a blender put the following: 1 pint mayonnaise, 2 tablespoons lemon juice, 1 large onion, chopped, 1 large green pepper, seeded and chopped and ½ teaspoon salt. Blend for several minutes until all ingredients are homogenized. Serve on mixed greens or vegetable salads.

CALIBOGUE CAFE
Hilton Head Island, South Carolina • illustration by Harvey Kidder

Pronounced "Calibogey," this is a colorful restaurant much favored by seafood lovers. It is in Sea Pines Plantation. Take U.S. Highway 278 to the island and follow signs to Harbourtown. Breakfast, lunch and dinner served daily. Kirk Bowker, the chef,

shares one of the restaurant's recipes, a Low Country special, for an unusual shrimp dish.

Pinkie's Shrimp Boil

3 pounds raw shrimp in shell	1 lemon, sliced
4 tablespoons butter	6 Oscar Mayer Little Smokies sausages
⅓ cup red and green bell peppers, diced	½ bay leaf
1 cup celery, diced fine	1 teaspoon Worcestershire sauce
1 cup onions, diced fine	Salt and pepper to taste
2 quarts chicken stock	
1½ tablespoons dry mustard	

In a large heavy pot melt butter and cook peppers, celery and onions, until soft but not brown. Add chicken stock and remaining ingredients, except shrimp, and let cook together for 5-10 minutes. Bring to a boil and add shrimp and cook for about 6 minutes. The local way of serving this dish is to ladle the shrimp without the cooking liquid into soup bowls. Makes 6 servings. Serve with hot bread and a tossed salad.

HUDSON'S SEAFOOD HOUSE
Hilton Head Island, South Carolina • illustration by Allen Palmer

Guests arrive by boat and car at this dockside restaurant at Skull Creek. It is on Hudson Road north of U.S. 278. Lunch and dinner served every day except Sunday. Closed the month of January. Brian and Gloria Carmines are the owners and managers.

Crab Cakes

1 pound white crabmeat	¼ teaspoon black pepper
4 slices white bread	

1 egg	1 tablespoon chopped
2 tablespoons	fresh parsley
mayonnaise	6 tablespoons butter
½ teaspoon dry mustard	

Crumble bread into fine crumbs. Combine all remaining ingredients except crab and butter in mixing bowl with crumbs. Gently fold in crabmeat, shape into 6 equal size patties. Sauté both sides in butter over medium heat until brown. Serves 6.

HACHLAND HILL
Clarksville, Tennessee • illustration by Gilbert DiCicco

Over 17 years ago Adolf and Phila Hach converted their magnificent 1790 southern mansion into a delightful country inn. There are roaring fires in the great fireplaces, fresh flowers on each table, and candlelight and soft music to make dinner here a memorable experience. The menu features true Southern cooking as well as dishes from all over the world. Breakfast, lunch and dinner served daily; reservations required. Overnight accommodations and party facilities. Closed only on Christmas day. The address is 1601 Madison (U.S. 41-A) at Tanglewood in Clarksville.

Buttermilk Lemon Pie

1 cup sugar	6 tablespoons lemon
9 tablespoons flour	juice
¼ teaspoon salt	1 baked pie shell
½ cup water	3 tablespoons sugar
2 cups buttermilk	beaten into 4 egg
4 egg yolks	whites for meringue
2 tablespoons butter	

Mix sugar, flour, salt, water and buttermilk, then cook in saucepan until thick, stirring constantly. Add

beaten egg yolks, butter and lemon juice. Cook a few minutes longer. Pour into pie shell, top with meringue and brown in 350° oven.

CATTLETOWN RESTAURANT
Richmond, Virginia • illustration by Jim Kelly

The Wild West is the theme of the three dining rooms at this delightful restaurant. There is a gourmet salad bar and open hearth broiling of steaks and barbecued ribs where diners can see their dinner being prepared. From I-64 take Broad Street Road exit, turn left and proceed east to 5205 West Broad Street. Lunch and dinner served daily 11:30 a.m. to 10:30 p.m. There is a Sunday chuck wagon buffet. Bob Harr and Richard Ripp are the owners.

Barbecued Spare Ribs

6 14-ounce racks baby	¼ cup black pepper
back pork ribs	1½ tablespoons paprika
½ cup salt	3 tablespoons MSG
½ cup sugar	Barbecue Sauce (below)
1½ tablespoons dry	
lemon powder	

Mix salt, sugar, lemon powder, pepper, paprika and MSG. Rub ribs generously on both sides with mixture. Place racks, bone side down, on baking pan. Bake at 425° for 30 minutes. Reduce heat to 300° and continue baking 3 to 4 hours or until very tender. Brush with barbecue sauce, return to oven for another 5 minutes. Serves 8.

Barbecue Sauce

3 tablespoons vinegar	2 teaspoons cayenne
3 tablespoons	pepper
Worcestershire sauce	1-2 tablespoons chili
2 tablespoons salt	powder
2 tablespoons sugar	3¼ cups ketchup
1-2 tablespoons paprika	2 cups water

Blend all ingredients in saucepan and simmer about 20 minutes or until slightly thickened. Correct seasonings, if necessary.

Western Barbecued Beans

Brown ¼ pound of ground beef in a heavy skillet. Add 20-ounce can of pork and beans, ½ cup ketchup, 1 teaspoon chili powder, 1 teaspoon sugar and ¼ teaspoon salt. Cook about 20 minutes until meat is tender and flavors are well blended. Serves 6.

Deep Dish Apple Pie

In a deep baking dish (1½ quart) combine 1¾ pounds sliced, canned apples with 1¼ cups sugar, 2 tablespoons cornstarch, and ¾ teaspoon each of cinnamon and nutmeg. Dot 2 tablespoons of butter over top of apple mixture. Place a pie crust over top of apples; wash with milk. Make slits with the point of knife. Sprinkle crust with cinnamon and sugar. Bake 30 minutes at 350°. Serve hot, topped with ice cream. Makes 8 portions.

BLUE PETE'S SEAFOOD RESTAURANT
Virginia Beach, Virginia • illustration by Robert Boston

Pat Ricks, the owner and cook, started out as a coach and teacher, but soon he and his wife, Betty Ann, decided they liked the restaurant business better. Their charming, rustic restaurant is outside Virginia Beach proper in the woods on Back Bay at 1365 North Muddy Creek Road. Dinner is served every day from 5:30 to 10 p.m.: reservations necessary. (Closed Monday and Tuesday in the winter.) The Rickses also operate a small craft shop that features handmade quilts, ceramics and paintings by local artists.

Sweet Potato Biscuits

2-3 medium sweet potatoes	1 teaspoon salt
½ cup butter or margarine	3½-4 cups all-purpose flour
½ cup sugar	4½ teaspoons baking powder
2 tablespoons milk	

Boil, peel and mash potatoes. While mashed potatoes are still hot, measure 1½ cups in a large bowl. Add butter, sugar, salt and milk. Mix well. Sift together flour and baking powder and add to potato mixture. Work with hands to make a soft dough. Chill dough, roll out and cut into biscuits. Bake on greased cookie sheet on top shelf of 400° oven for 15-20 minutes until light golden brown. Makes 12 biscuits.

MILTON WARREN'S ICE HOUSE RESTAURANT
Virginia Beach, Virginia • illustration by Marcus Hamilton

The building that houses this restaurant dates back to the turn of the century and was once the city ice house. The owner and host is Milton Warren. Open for dinner every day during the summer; closed on Sunday from Labor Day to Memorial Day. Reservations accepted. To reach the restaurant go south on Pacific Avenue in Virginia Beach, turn right onto Norfolk Avenue and continue west for three blocks to 604 Norfolk Avenue.

Mushroom Crab Broil

Wash 16 extra-large, fresh mushrooms and remove stems. Place caps (cap-side up) on a broiler pan, brush with butter and broil 3-4 minutes or until mushrooms turn brown. Chop mushroom stems and sauté in butter. Mix 2 eggs, 2 tablespoons Durkee's Famous Sauce, 6 drops Tabasco, 1 tablespoon horseradish, ¼ teaspoon salt, ⅛ teaspoon pepper and 1 tablespoon chopped parsley. Separate 1 pound fresh backfin crabmeat by hand and pour egg mixture into crabmeat. Add sautéed mushroom stems. Mix lightly. Stuff mushroom caps with the crab mixture, brush melted butter on the top and broil for about 5 minutes or until crab mixture turns golden brown. Serves 8 as an entree.

OLD BUDAPEST HUNGARIAN RESTAURANT

Martinsburg, West Virginia • illustration by Frank Saso

Authentic Hungarian cuisine is served with Old World courtesy in this popular restaurant owned by Mr. and Mrs. John Taba. It is six miles north of Martinsburg, on U.S. 11, or take Exit 5 from Interstate 81. Lunch and dinner served daily from 11 a.m. to 11 p.m.; Saturday, dinner only. Closed on Monday. Reservations advisable on weekends.

Stuffed Cabbage

Cut out center core of a large head of white cabbage. Put cored cabbage in a large pot, pour boiling water over it and let stand until leaves are wilted. Remove leaves, set aside and make filling.

Filling

Combine 2 pounds lean ground pork, 4 egg yolks, 2 teaspoons salt, 1 tablespoon medium hot paprika, ½ cup chopped onions, 1 teaspoon finely ground pepper and ½ cup raw rice. Fill leaves with stuffing mixture, roll up and fasten with toothpicks.

Divide 2 pounds of sauerkraut into 3 parts. Place a third of the sauerkraut on the bottom of a cooking dish and sprinkle with a tablespoon of olive oil, a pinch of caraway seed and a crumbled bay leaf. Place half of the rolls on top, repeat sauerkraut layer and

seasonings, then add another layer of cabbage rolls. Place remaining sauerkraut on top, add same seasonings. Sprinkle with 2 tablespoons of red paprika. Bake in a 300° oven for 1 hour. Top with sour cream. Serves 6.

GRANNY'S SANDWITCHERY

Parkersburg, West Virginia • illustration by Don McGovern

Constance Harris is the owner of this charming small restaurant that prides itself on its unusual menu of sandwiches at lunch and fine Continental cuisine in the evening. Lunch and dinner are served every day except Monday. Reservations necessary. Closed first two weeks in January. It is at 1714 16th Street in Parkersburg. Take the downtown exit from U.S. 77.

Pineapple Cake

2 cups flour	2 teaspoons soda
2 cups crushed	2 eggs
pineapple, undrained	1 cup walnuts, chopped
2 cups sugar	

Stir all ingredients together well. Pour into greased 9 x 12 pan, and bake in 350° oven until done (about 40 minutes). When cool frost with icing (below).

Icing

8 ounces cream cheese	1½-2 cups confectioners'
½ cup butter	sugar
	1 tablespoon vanilla

Whip the cream cheese and butter together. Add sugar and vanilla.

PIPESTEM RESORT
Pipestem, West Virginia • illustration by Robert Curran Smith

This fine family resort complex is set in the heart of a state park in the Appalachians. There are excellent dining rooms in the lodges and a magnificent campground nearby. In addition to an 18 hole championship golf course there are swimming pools, horses, lakes for fishing and a health club. Breakfast, lunch and dinner served daily. Reservations advisable for overnight accommodations. It is on State Highway 20, midway between Princeton and Hinton.

Chicken Marengo

Cut 2 frying chickens into serving pieces and season with salt and pepper. Cover with milk and marinate for 2 hours at room temperature. Drain and dry chicken and dredge in seasoned flour. Sauté chicken in mixture of ½ pound of butter, ½ cup of olive oil and ½ garlic clove, diced fine. When chicken is lightly browned remove from the fire and the pan. Sauté together in butter used to brown chicken: 2 diced green peppers, 1 onion, diced, and 5 whole fresh or canned tomatoes, diced. Quarter 2½ pounds of fresh mushrooms and finely chop 1 bunch of parsley. Arrange chicken, mushrooms, parsley and sautéed vegetables in alternate layers in a casserole. Reserve cooking oil. Cover casserole and bake for 1 hour. When chicken is done add salt, pepper and 4 ounces of sherry to cooking oil. Heat and pour over chicken casserole. Makes 6 portions.

COUNTRY ROAD INN
Summersville, West Virginia • illustration by William Boisvenue

Family-style home-cooked meals in a farmhouse of the pre-Civil War days is the big attraction of this restaurant located near the Carnifax Ferry Battlegrounds. Owners Janet and David Jarroll

specialize in Italian cuisine. The homemade pastas and antipastos made by Mrs. Jarroll have served to spread the restaurant's fame throughout the area. Open for dinner by reservations only from 5 to 9 o'clock daily except Christmas Eve and Day and New Year's Day. Nearby attractions include Summersville Lake with camping facilities and the New River Gorge Bridge. Closest main highways are I-79 and U.S. 19.

Chicken Scaloppine

3 whole chicken breasts, split	1 green pepper, sliced
3 tablespoons cooking oil	1 medium onion, sliced
1½ teaspoons salt	12 fresh mushrooms, sliced
	1 cup dry white wine

Remove skin from chicken breasts and pound to flatten. Heat oil in large skillet. Add chicken and sauté on both sides until lightly browned. Sprinkle with salt. Add green pepper, onion and mushrooms. Sauté lightly. Add wine, cover and simmer slowly until tender. Serves 6.

HOTEL ROSE HALL
Montego Bay, Jamaica • illustration by Leonard Johnson

On a 30-acre beach front, this luxurious Intercontinental hotel is surrounded by a sugar estate, with its legendary Great House, reputedly haunted by the ghost of its former mistress. Each of the 500 rooms has a balcony overlooking the ocean and the hotel has its own 18-hole golf course which starts at sea level, rising to over 300 feet elevation. Breakfast, lunch and dinner served daily in six dining rooms. There are complete recreation and convention facilities. Reservations necessary.

Lobster Savannah

6 cooked, medium-size lobsters or lobster tails	1 lemon, juice
	4 raw eggs, beaten
1 cup Béchamel sauce (white sauce)	3 ounces Parmesan cheese
1½ teaspoons dry mustard	6 ounces bread crumbs
	Salt and pepper, to taste
½ clove garlic, chopped	6 ounces melted butter

Cut cooked lobster or lobster tails in half and break out meat. Clean shells and keep for refilling. Cut lobster meat in ¼-inch cubes. Combine Béchamel sauce, mustard, garlic, lemon juice and eggs and fold into lobster chunks. Split filling into 6 equal parts and refill shells with the mixture. Sprinkle bread crumbs and Parmesan cheese over filled shells and bake in 375° oven for 20 minutes. Serve hot with melted butter and lemon wedges. Serves 6.

Real Jamaican Pepperpot — the Dowry Soup

In days gone by, a good Jamaican cook had a special pot simmering by the fire just for Pepperpot Soup. Fresh ingredients were added daily so that the bottom of the pot was never seen. So prized were these that many new brides took their mother's pot with them as part of their dowry. Today it remains one of the most popular soups in Jamaica.

½ pound each: spinach, kale and okra, or any similar green vegetables	2 quarts water
	2 large potatoes, diced
	½ pound yam, diced
	2 large green onions, chopped
½ pound pigs' tails	1 hot pepper
¼ pound salt beef, or stewing beef	Salt and pepper, to taste
2 cups coconut milk	

Boil green vegetables and meat until tender. Remove vegetables from pot and purée, then return to pot with meat. Add potatoes, yam, onion and pepper. Simmer for about 30 minutes. Add salt and pepper, to taste. Serve hot. Makes 6 portions.

SIGN GREAT HOUSE

Montego Bay, Jamaica • illustration from Jamaica Tourist Board

A refurbished 200-year-old plantation offers guests tennis, horseback riding, swimming in a garden-side pool plus fishing and boating on a private lake. The dining room features Jamaican dishes, and nightly entertainment. Dining is open to those not staying at the resort. Reservations are necessary. Donald Hacker is the general manager.

Red Pea Soup — Jamaica Style

2 cups red peas (red pea beans)	½ pound sweet potatoes, sliced
½ pound pigs' tails, chopped	1½ teaspoons thyme leaf
	3 scallions, chopped
½ pound salt beef or pork, cubed	1 large onion, diced
	¼ hot red pepper
1 pound stewing beef, cubed	
½ pound potatoes, cubed	

Boil peas with meat in 4 quarts of water for 1 hour, or until peas are soft. Add remaining ingredients and simmer for another hour or more, removing pepper after 10 minutes. Skim fat and season to taste. Serves 6.

North Central

Choucroute Garnie – Pontchartrain Wine Cellars, Michigan
Black Forest Torte – Shields, Michigan
Old-Fashioned Corn Bread – Iron Duke, Minnesota
Broiled Whitefish with Cucumber Sauce – Big Bay Hotel, Michigan

DON ROTH'S
BLACKHAWK RESTAURANT
Chicago, Illinois • illustration by William Boisvenue

A downtown landmark since 1920 when it was founded by the owner's father, this restaurant is famous for roast beef, hearth-broiled steaks and the spinning salad bowl. It is also nostalgically known as the home of many big bands that broadcast music to the nation. Located at 139 North Wabash Avenue near the Loop, it is popular for lunch and dinner. Reservations suggested.

Spinning Salad Bowl

3 ounces cream cheese, softened
3 ounces blue cheese, crumbled
5 to 6 tablespoons water
1 egg
4½ teaspoons lemon juice
1 cup vegetable oil
¼ cup red wine vinegar
¼ teaspoon prepared mustard
¾ teaspoon paprika
¾ teaspoon salt
¼ teaspoon garlic powder
½ teaspoon white pepper
1 tablespoon sugar
2 tablespoons snipped chives
2 tablespoons salad-sandwich sauce (Durkee)
1½ teaspoons Worcestershire sauce
Salad greens, hard-cooked egg, seasoned salt, pepper, 8 anchovy filets

Beat cheeses until smooth. Gradually beat in water until of pouring consistency. Set aside. Place egg, lemon juice, ¼ cup oil in blender. Blend at medium 15 seconds. Increase speed. Slowly add remaining oil. Add vinegar, mustard, seasonings, sugar, chives and sauces. Blend until smooth. In salad bowl mix greens (4 parts lettuce, 2 parts romaine, 1 part endive). Pour in enough dressing to coat greens.

Sprinkle with salt, pepper and chopped egg. Toss gently 3 times. Garnish with anchovies. Serves 4 to 6. Tip: Remaining dressing and cheese may be refrigerated and stored up to 2 weeks.

LE BASTILLE RESTAURANT FRANCAIS
Chicago, Illinois • illustration by Norris MacNamara

George Badonsky presides over this French bistro at 21 West Superior off North Michigan Avenue. A fine wine cellar is maintained. Lunch and dinner are served 11:30 to 11:30, Monday through Friday. Dinner from 5:30 to 11:30, Saturday and Sunday. Closed on Sunday. Reservations are necessary.

Veau Sauté Normande

30 ounces loin of veal, sliced thin
1 cup seasoned flour
3 tablespoons unsalted butter
2 tablespoons olive oil
1 ounce good applejack (apple brandy)
6 fresh mushrooms, sliced
½ lemon, juice
1 teaspoon veal or chicken stock
½ cup whipping cream
1 teaspoon fines herbes (mixed herbs)
1 tablespoon chopped parsley

Pound veal slices until they are very thin. Dredge in flour seasoned with salt and pepper. Sauté floured veal in oil and butter. Cook briefly on both sides — the veal should be rare. Pour applejack into pan. Remove veal, keep hot. Put mushroom slices and lemon juice into the same pan and sauté. Add whipping cream and veal or chicken stock and cook gently to reduce. Sprinkle with *fines herbes* and parsley and pour over hot veal slices. Garnish with baked apple slices (below). Makes 6 portions.

Baked Apple Slices

Peel and core 3 apples. Cut in quarters, then slices, keeping slices together. Sprinkle with sugar and melted butter. Pour water into the bottom of a baking pan and place in 350° oven for about a half hour.

THE RITZ-CARLTON HOTEL
Chicago, Illinois • illustration by Gilbert DiCicco

On Chicago's fashionable near north side at the Water Tower Place, a block-square commercial-retail-residential complex, this elegant hotel and its dining rooms carry on a proud culinary tradition. The original chef of the Paris Ritz was Auguste Escoffier and many of his original recipes are used in The Dining Room of this new hotel. Lunch is served from noon to 2:30, dinner from 6 to 11:30. Reservations necessary. The address is 160 East Pearson Street.

Crepes à la Ritz

Make your favorite crepes (enough to serve 10) and flavor with grated orange rind and Grand Marnier.

Pastry Cream

Blend together 6 eggs, 4 tablespoons flour and 1 cup of sugar until mixture is creamy. Bring 2 cups of milk to the boiling point with 2 drops of almond extract and 2 drops of vanilla. Pour hot milk over egg mixture, stirring well. When milk is blended, pour back into pan and bring to a gentle boiling point, stirring constantly. Cook for 5 minutes. Cool in refrigerator in a flat pan. When cream is cold, blend with two 8-ounce cans of almond filling paste. Fill crepes with this mixture and fold. Top with chocolate sauce (below).

Chocolate Sauce

Bring 4 ounces simple sugar syrup and 4 ounces whipping cream to boiling point. Crumble 8 ounces sweet baking chocolate and 8 ounces bitter chocolate into small pieces in the top of a double boiler and let melt over hot water. Place filled crepes on a buttered serving platter and heat in a 350° oven for 10 minutes. Flame with hot cognac. Stir hot chocolate sauce and pour over crepes. Garnish with toasted, sliced almonds.

THE WHITEHALL HOTEL
Chicago, Illinois • illustration by Larry McManus

This small, luxurious hotel is located in the Water Tower area of the north side of Chicago at 105 East Delaware Place. The famous old Whitehall Club is quartered here. The hotel features a variety of accommodations, from large single rooms to spectacular suites. Kevin Lloyd Molloy is vice-president and general manager. Dinner reservations advisable.

Medaillon de Veau Oscar

8 round slices veal loin, 4 ounces each	*1 medium shallot, minced*
Salt, pepper and flour	*12 ounces king crab meat*
6 tablespoons butter	*Béarnaise sauce (page 62)*
8 pieces asparagus, 5 inches long	*Chopped parsley*
3 ounces white wine	

Season veal slices with salt and pepper and sprinkle with flour. Sauté in butter 3 to 4 minutes on each side over medium high heat until slightly browned. Set aside and keep warm. Cook asparagus in salted boiling water until just crisp, about 5 minutes. Keep warm. Heat wine, shallots and crab meat, bring to boiling, set aside and keep warm. Place 2 medallions on each serving plate. Top with crab meat mixture. Place an asparagus stalk on each side, then cover with Béarnaise sauce and sprinkle with parsley. Serves 4.

Béarnaise Sauce

2 tablespoons chopped shallots	1 cup white wine
¼ teaspoon crushed white peppercorns	2 pinches salt
	½ cup vinegar
½ teaspoon tarragon leaves	4 egg yolks
	16 ounces clarified butter

Place shallots, peppercorns, tarragon, wine, salt and vinegar in small saucepan. Cook slowly until liquid is nearly evaporated. Strain through cheesecloth and set aside to cool. Place 4 egg yolks in bowl, add strained liquid and place over boiling water. Whip vigorously until eggs foam up. Pour clarified butter in a small steady stream, beating constantly until mixture thickens and forms soft peaks.

JUMER'S CASTLE LODGE
Peoria, Illinois • illustration by Randall McKissick

Old world elegance describes the unique Bavarian Castle Lodge perched on a high bluff, overlooking Peoria's Illinois River valley. The owner, D. James Jumer, has assembled a priceless collection of antiques and German artifacts to complement the fine German-American food served from 7 a.m. to midnight daily. Located at Western and Moss, the Lodge is five minutes from either downtown Peoria or the airport. Reservations required.

Sauerbraten

6 pounds boneless beef roast	4 tablespoons sugar
4 ounces melted suet	2 tablespoons wine vinegar

¼ cup sherry	Dash white pepper
½ ounce ground pickling spices	1 cup crushed gingersnaps

Place meat in crock, pour in cooled brine marinade (below) and let stand in refrigerator 5 days, turning twice daily. When ready to cook remove meat from marinade, drain and pat dry. Slowly brown in heavy pan on all sides in hot suet, about 1 hour. Add sugar, vinegar, sherry, pepper and pickling spices. Brown 10 minutes longer. Strain marinade and pour 2 cups over meat. Simmer, uncovered, 3 hours, adding beef stock or water and more marinade as needed. Remove meat, skim off fat and thicken gravy with crushed gingersnaps. If a thicker gravy is desired, thicken with flour and water. Serves 12.

Brine Marinade

Mix and bring to boiling 8 ounces wine vinegar; 1 quart water; 1 large onion, sliced; 1 stalk celery, chopped; 1 carrot, sliced; 1 ounce pickling spices; 2 tablespoons salt; 1 bay leaf; 1 cup Burgundy wine; 1 tablespoon garlic powder and a pinch of ginger. Cool and pour over meat.

MURPHY'S ROMEO CAFE
Romeoville, Illinois • illustration by John Small

The little village of Romeoville boasts one of the most popular restaurants in the Joliet area, Murphy's, which is located on 135th Street, a half mile east of State Highway 53, about 35 miles from the Chicago Loop. It's an informal family roadside inn where meals are cooked to order. Open for dinner Wednesday through Sunday. Reservations are necessary.

Watercress Soup

3 leeks, chopped	4 tablespoons butter
1 onion, chopped	3 raw potatoes, sliced

3 cups chicken stock
1 bunch watercress
1 cup milk

1 cup half and half cream
1 teaspoon salt
Whipped cream for
  garnish

Sauté leeks and onion in butter. Add potatoes and chicken stock. Cook until tender, about 45 minutes. Boil watercress in salted water for 2 minutes. Drain and put in blender with leek and onion mixture. Add milk, cream and salt. Serve hot or cold with a dollop of whipped cream on each cup. Serves 8.

Pecan Pie

With an electric mixer add 2½ cups light corn syrup to ⅓ cup flour and ⅓ cup light brown sugar. Blend until smooth. Add 5 large eggs, one at a time, blending well. Take off mixer, stir in 2 tablespoons melted butter, 2 teaspoons vanilla and 1 cup pecans. Pour into unbaked 10-inch pie shell. Bake at 350° about 40 minutes or until filling begins to rise in the center.

IMPERIAL CROWN RESTAURANT
Columbus, Indiana • illustration by Kermit Oliver

This Imperial House Motel restaurant specializes in a gourmet French-American menu. It is located in Columbus on State Highway 46, just a short distance east of I-65. Breakfast, a lunch buffet from 11 to 2, and dinner are served in the dining room every day. Overnight accommodations and vacation facilities offered in the motel.

Spanish Coffee

Light a Sterno can. Take 2 large wine glasses and turn brims in an orange half. Dip wine glass in granulated sugar so the brim is frosted. Turn glasses over flame until sugar crystalizes. Put 2 tablespoons brown sugar in each glass. Heat 2 ounces Irish whiskey over flame, then light it. Pour flaming whiskey over the brown sugar in each glass (moving the glasses will keep it burning). Pour 1 ounce of Kahlua in each glass. Stir, then fill with black coffee until 2 inches from the top. Put whipped cream on the top. Tie a napkin around the stem of glass and serve. Can be served either as a dessert or an after-dinner drink.

F'S STEAK HOUSE
Evansville, Indiana • illustration by Frederick Browning

From U.S. Highway 41 take the Walnut Street exit to downtown and 125 S. E. Fourth Street. Mrs. Eleanor Crow has owned and managed this homey restaurant for the past 30 years. It is noted for its excellent steaks and chops, and Chinese food prepared by five chefs from Canton, China. Lunch and dinner served weekdays from 11 a.m. to midnight. Reservations necessary.

Maggie Murphy Casserole

6 6-ounce lean pork
  chops
6 medium-size raw
  potatoes, sliced ½-
  inch thick

1 large Spanish onion,
  sliced thin
2 10¾-ounce cans cream
  of tomato soup
Salt and pepper, to taste

In a medium-size casserole, alternate layers of sliced potatoes and onions, seasoning each layer with salt and pepper. Continue until casserole is about three-quarters full. Place pork chops on top. Combine soup with 1 can of water, stir well and pour over casserole. Cover and bake at 325° for 1½ hours; uncover and bake for 20 minutes to brown top. Serves 6.

OVERLOOK RESTAURANT
Leavenworth, Indiana • illustration by Robert Taylor

The dining room is perched on a bluff overlooking the Ohio River, 32 miles west of Louisville. It is a great place to dine and also to watch barges come up the river or see the sun set behind the hills in Kentucky. It is on State Highway 62 (The Lincoln Heritage Trail) in southern Indiana. Open for breakfast, lunch and dinner every day. Closed Christmas Eve and Christmas. It is near a marina, and there are three caves for travelers to explore within 12 miles of the restaurant.

Dang Good Pie

¾ *stick butter or*	*1 cup crushed*
magarine	*pineapple, drained*
3 eggs	*1 cup coconut flakes*
3 tablespoons flour	*9-inch unbaked pie shell*
1½ cups sugar	

Melt butter and mix with remaining ingredients. Pour filling into unbaked pie shell and bake 1 hour at 350° or until set and brown.

THE RED GERANIUM
New Harmony, Indiana • illustration by Michael W. Green

This charming restaurant in the restored town of New Harmony was built in 1814 by Father George Rapp and his followers who were known as Rappites or Harmonists, an industrious group of craftsmen and workers who remained in the community until 1824. Twenty-five of their buildings remain in the historic town today. The restaurant serves lunch and dinner every day except Monday. Reservations necessary. Overnight accommodations available in the adjacent New Harmony Inn. It is on North Street, one block north of State Highway 66 in the center of town.

Filet Wellington

3 pounds center-cut beef	*1 ounce sherry*
filet	*1 tablespoon tomato*
2 tablespoons melted	*paste*
butter	*1 egg yolk*
¼ pound mushrooms,	*2 tablespoons water*
chopped fine	*1 flaky pie crust*
½ pound ground cooked	
ham	
1½ tablespoons butter	

Brush filet with butter. Brown well on all sides in a hot oven for 10-15 minutes. Sauté mushrooms and ham together in butter, add sherry and tomato paste. Mix well. Place beef filet in center of rolled-out, chilled pie crust. Top beef filet with ham and mushroom mixture. Wrap beef filet with pastry. Seal. Combine egg yolk and water and brush pastry. Bake 20 minutes at 425° for medium. Slice and serve with Béarnaise or Bordelaise sauce. Serves 6.

MORRIS BRYANT SMORGASBORD
West Lafayette, Indiana • illustration by Harvey Kidder

In addition to featuring a lavish breakfast, lunch and dinner buffet every day, this fine eating place offers a champagne brunch every Sunday. Closed Monday. It is four miles northwest of Lafayette at 1800 U.S. Highway 52, West.

Swedish Rice Pudding

½ cup uncooked rice	*2 cups milk*
¼ cup crushed	*½ teaspoon vanilla*
pineapple	*Drop of yellow color*
3 tablespoons sugar	*Grape jelly or preserves*
2 eggs	

Cook rice and combine with crushed pineapple and set aside. Add sugar to eggs, while mixing at slow speed. Add milk, vanilla and yellow food coloring to eggs while mixing. Pour rice and pineapple in egg mixture. Pour into greased pan so that mixture is about one-inch deep. Bake at 375° for two hours. Serve hot or cold, topped with grape jelly or preserves. Serves 10.

EL RANCHO VILLA
Bettendorf, Iowa • illustration by Robert Boston

Mr. and Mrs. Irvin French are the owners of this friendly restaurant at 2211 Kimberly Road in northwest Bettendorf, a quarter mile south of I-74. Breakfast, lunch and dinner served every day except Sunday. Reservations necessary.

Villa Luncheon Salad

6 medium-sized chicken breasts	1 small onion
	1 bay leaf
1 cup finely chopped celery	Salad dressing, to bind
	½ cup toasted almonds
1 cup drained pineapple tidbits	Shredded lettuce

Poach chicken breasts in enough water to cover, add onion, sliced, and the bay leaf. Cool and refrigerate in poaching liquid overnight. Cut chicken in cubes and combine with remaining ingredients, except nuts and lettuce. Mix thoroughly and place on bed of shredded lettuce. Top salad with a sprinkling of toasted almonds. Serves 12.

Villa Supreme Sandwich

8 generous slices of turkey	8 slices sharp Cheddar cheese
4 slices of toast	8 slices crisp bacon
2 cups chicken base cream sauce	

Place turkey slices on hot buttered toast, top with cream sauce and cheese slices. Place under hot broiler just long enough to melt cheese. Top each open-faced sandwich with 2 slices crisp bacon. Serves 4.

STEAK HOUSE
Hawarden, Iowa • illustration by Fred Browning

Dorothy and Jim Skogman are the hosts at this 50-year-old restaurant which specializes in fine aged steaks and chops. Dinner is served every day except Sunday and Monday. Also closed first two weeks in January and the week of Labor Day. Reservations necessary for large groups only. The address is 711 Center Avenue.

65

Vegetable Macaroni Salad

1 pound macaroni
1 large green pepper,
    chopped
1 chopped onion
4 shredded carrots
1 can Eagle Brand
    Condensed Milk

1 cup vinegar
1 cup sugar
2 cups mayonnaise
1 teaspoon salt and ¼
    teaspoon pepper

Cook macaroni, drain and cool. Add vegetables and mix well. Combine milk, vinegar, sugar, mayonnaise, salt and pepper. Add these ingredients to macaroni mixture. Mix thoroughly and chill at least 4 hours before serving. Makes 10 portions.

Meat Rolls

2 pounds lean ground
    beef
1 cup water
1 teaspoon pepper
¼ teaspoon onion salt

½ teaspoon garlic salt
4 tablespoons seasoned
    meat tenderizer
½ teaspoon mustard
    seed

Mix all ingredients together and refrigerate overnight. Form into two one-inch rolls. Wrap in foil and bake 1 hour in 350° oven. Slice and serve cold with assorted crackers. Makes 10 to 12 servings.

CLANCY'S
Lansing, Iowa • illustration by Max Altekruse

"Iowa's finest food" is the boast of this popular eating place which has many awards. It is located in a beautiful resort area of the upper Mississippi River, known as the "Little Switzerland of Iowa," which is famous for bass and pike fishing. The Clancy family who own and operate this establishment began their business in 1933. It is open for dinner 5 p.m. to midnight, Tuesday through Saturday. The address is 420 Main Street— a half block east of the intersection of State Highways 9 and 182.

Salisbury Steak

Mix 5 pounds lean ground beef, salt and fresh pepper (to taste), 3 ounces Heinz 57 Sauce, 2 ounces Bovril or other beef extract, 2 ounces Ac'cent and ¼ pound soft butter. Mix thoroughly and shape into 8-ounce patties. Grill at moderate temperature. Top each portion with beef juice and a couple of butter pats. This dish can also be served with cheese, mushroom or tomato sauce. Makes 10 portions.

Celery Seed Dressing

Mix 2½ cups white sugar, ½ cup brown sugar, 3 tablespoons salt, 1 teaspoon white pepper, ½ cup ketchup, ¼ cup lemon juice, 3 tablespoons celery seed and 1 teaspoon ground sweet basil. Add 1 pint sauterne wine vinegar with tarragon. Mix again. Put 1 cup of oil and 6 teaspoons tragacanth (available from a druggist) in a separate, covered jar and shake. Add ½ cup water and shake again. Slowly add 3 cups of oil to the first mixture. Stir slowly while pouring. Then add the oil with tragacanth.

STRAWTOWN INN
Pella, Iowa • illustration by Roy Pauli

Special European dinners are served in the main dining room of this restored 1855 home, one of the first built by the area's Dutch settlers. There is also a cozy wine cellar where dinner and sandwiches are offered. Lunch and dinner served every day, except Sunday and Monday evenings. Reservations necessary for meals. About 40 miles southeast of Des Moines, it is at 1111 Washington Street (State Highway 163) at the west end of Pella.

Stuffed Pork Chops

*3-pound boneless pork
    loin, cut into six 8-
    ounce portions*

Make a pocket in the six chops and stuff each with dressing (below). Place in baking pan and put ¼ inch water or pork stock in bottom of pan, cover with foil and roast at 250° for 3 hours. Serves 6.

Dressing

Mix together lightly 8 cups sweet dough bread, ⅓ cup chopped celery, ⅓ cup diced apple, ⅓ cup chopped onion, ⅓ cup chopped English walnuts, ½ teaspoon salt, ½ teaspoon paprika and 1 teaspoon chopped parsley. Stir ingredients while adding milk until all ingredients are just moist.

LAKEWOOD INN

Battle Creek, Michigan • illustration by Richard A. Young

Built on the site of an old Indian Village, this inn overlooks Goguac Lake, named after the prairie which surrounds it. Open for lunch and dinner every day; closed most holidays. Reservations advisable. From I-94 take Capital Avenue Exit north to the first traffic light, go west on Columbia and proceed 400 yards to the inn.

Regal Rack of Lamb

*1 five-pound lamb rack
1 quart sherry wine
¼ cup lemon juice
2 cups water
1 teaspoon rosemary
    leaves*

*¼ teaspoon garlic
    granules, or 2 cloves
    crushed fresh garlic
½ teaspoon salt*

Trim the rack of lamb down to just the eye of the rack. Cut in between the ribs about 2 inches down. Then marinate lamb in a mixture of the remaining ingredients for 24-28 hours before roasting. Remove

from marinade, brown rack under broiler, then place in 425° oven for 20-25 minutes. Serves 4.

BAY VALLEY INN

Bay City, Michigan • illustration by Jan Cicala

A four season vacation complex, this inn has indoor-outdoor tennis courts and swimming pools, an 18-hole championship golf course, and many other recreation facilities. The dining rooms are open daily for breakfast, lunch and dinner. Reservations necessary for dinner and for overnight accommodation. It is just off I-75, south of Bay City (take the M-84 exit) at 2470 Old Bridge Road.

Bay Valley Shrimp Bisque

*1 pound raw shrimp,
    diced
¼ cup celery, minced
    fine
2 shallots, minced fine
1 garlic clove, minced
    fine
¼ pound butter
½ cup flour
1 tablespoon paprika*

*1 pint heavy cream
1 pint fish stock or clam
    broth
½ teaspoon ground
    pickling spice
¼ teaspoon dry English
    mustard
Salt and white pepper
½ cup dry sherry*

Sauté shrimp, celery, shallots and garlic in butter until transparent. Add flour and paprika. Cook over low heat 5 minutes, stirring slowly to make a roux. Add cream, fish stock, spice and mustard to roux, stir and simmer to smooth boiling point. Add salt and pepper to taste. Remove from heat, fold in sherry and serve in heated cups. Serves 6.

BIG BAY HOTEL

Big Bay, Michigan • illustration by Dennis Bellile

Formerly a small general store, this building was purchased by Henry Ford in 1944 and transformed

into a hotel complete with a colonial entrance. Mr. Ford visited here many times on business trips to the Upper Peninsula. Later, the hotel was sold to the present owners, Mr. and Mrs. C. B. Stortz. In 1959, Otto Preminger decided to film some of the scenes for the film *Anatomy of a Murder* at the hotel and he added another wing and even changed the name for a short time. Today it is a favorite rustic dining spot and hotel in the north woods village of Big Bay, 28 miles northwest of Marquette. Open for breakfast, lunch and dinner. Reservations advisable for meals and 17 guest rooms.

Broiled Whitefish with Cucumber Sauce

2 pounds whitefish or	*Paprika*
lake trout	*3 bay leaves*
1 fresh lemon	

Broil fish in ¼ inch of water. Lightly sprinkle paprika on fish and squeeze lemon juice over it. Add bay leaves to water. Serve with cucumber sauce, below. Makes 6 portions.

Cucumber Sauce

Bring 2 tablespoons butter to a bubbly boil, quickly stir in 2 tablespoons sifted flour with whip, then set aside. Bring 1 cup milk to a boil, stirring constantly on low heat. When just at a boil, stir in butter mixture and season with salt and pepper. Cut cucumber into quarters, the long way; remove seeds. Puree sauce and cucumber together in a blender. Cut 3 small tomatoes in half and scoop out pulp and fill with sauce. Sprinkle with paprika and garnish with parsley. Serve with fish.

Lemon Chiffon Pie with Buttercrunch Crust

Crust

Mix together ½ cup chopped pecans, 1 cup flour,

¼ cup brown sugar and ½ cup soft butter. Place in a 9 x 12-inch pan and bake at 400° for 15 minutes. Remove from oven and stir mixture. Reserve ½ cup for topping, press remainder firmly in a 9-inch pie pan. Refrigerate until filling is ready.

Filling

To prepare filling combine contents of 3-ounce package of Jello lemon chiffon pie mix (or instant lemon pudding mix), ½ cup sugar, and ¼ cup water in saucepan. Stir in 2 egg yolks, then stir in 1½ cups water. Cook and stir over medium heat to full boil, about 5 minutes, remove from heat and stir in ¼ cup lemon juice and grated rind of one lemon. Beat 2 egg whites until foamy and gradually add ¼ cup sugar, beating until stiff. Slowly fold hot pudding into egg whites and pour into chilled crust. Refrigerate about 4-6 hours. Before serving, pour 1 cup whipping cream in a bowl and whip until it thickens. Continue beating, slowly adding 2 teaspoons sugar and ½ teaspoon vanilla. Spread on pie. Sprinkle with reserved crumb mixture.

Broccoli Potato

Spread open 2 hot, baked potatoes. Dot with butter. Place 12 ounces fresh, partially-cooked broccoli on shaped and buttered potatoes. Make 1 cup of white sauce, then add 2 ounces each of grated Swiss and mild Cheddar cheese. Pour cheese sauce over broccoli and top with tomato slices. Sprinkle top liberally with grated Parmesan cheese and place in 350° oven for about 10-15 minutes to melt cheese. Can be served as an entree or as a vegetable course.

HATHAWAY HOUSE

Blissfield, Michigan • illustration by Richard A. Young

For 15 years the Arthur Weeber family has operated this charming restaurant in a 125-year-old Greek Revival style home, a Michigan Historical Site. There are six beautiful dining rooms, with five fireplaces. Lunch and dinner served every day except Monday; special smorgasbord on Sunday from 11:30 a.m. to 4 p.m. Reservations advisable. On U.S. 223 in town, it is 10 miles west of U.S. 23 about halfway between Adrian, Michigan, and Toledo, Ohio.

Carrot Marmalade

5 large carrots
2 whole lemons
4 cups sugar
½ cup chopped walnuts (optional)

Grind carrots and lemons (rind included) together, add sugar and mix well. Let mixture stand in refrigerator overnight so a good syrup forms. Simmer the following day until carrot bits are tender. Add walnuts if desired and store in refrigerator. Makes about a quart. Serve on hot biscuits with a chicken dinner.

DEARBORN INN
Dearborn, Michigan • illustration by Robert Boston

Henry Ford built the Dearborn Inn in 1931 for the convenient accommodation of travelers who landed at the nearby Ford airport. Today this charming colonial hostelry on Oakwood Boulevard is just a few hundred feet from the Henry Ford Museum, Greenfield Village and the Ford Guest Center. Information on special Early-American-Weekend packages available on request. Breakfast, lunch and dinner served daily. Overnight accommodations and vacation facilities. Reservations advisable. Adrian deVogel is the manager.

Veal Chops, Hunter's Style

Season 8 one-inch veal chops with salt and pepper and then roll in flour until they are coated lightly. Brown chops slowly in a sauté pan in 4 tablespoons of olive oil. Remove browned chops from pan. Into the pan put 8 tablespoons of butter and sauté 24 floured chicken livers. Remove livers and keep warm. In the same pan cook 4 teaspoons mixed, finely chopped onion and mushrooms until brown. Add 1 cup white wine and cook until liquid is reduced by half. To this mixture add 2 cups brown gravy and 2 cups thin tomato sauce. Return chops and chicken livers to the pan and place in 300° oven for 30 minutes or until meat is tender. Serve over 4 cups of hot buttered noodles which have been seasoned with ½ cup of grated Parmesan cheese. Makes 8 servings.

KYOTO JAPANESE STEAK HOUSE
Dearborn, Michigan • illustration by Max Altekruse

Steaks, seafood, chicken and vegetables are specialties prepared at the table on Teppan grills by skilled Japanese chefs. The dining room is open every day for dinner; Monday through Saturday for lunch; reservations advisable. At 18601 Hubbard Drive, it is adjacent to Fairlane Town Center, a half mile north of Michigan Avenue. Manager Koji Watanabe is a native of Hiroshima.

Kyoto Onion Soup

12 cups chicken-beef stock
1 teaspoon each salt and pepper
1 teaspoon soy sauce
2 ounces sliced mushrooms
1 ounce green onion
5 ounces deep-fried, sliced onion

To make stock combine chicken and beef bones and water in a large kettle and let simmer for 5 hours. Season with salt, pepper and soy sauce. Remove bones, then strain so that only clear broth remains. Divide remaining ingredients in 8 bowls, pour hot broth over ingredients and serve. Makes 8 portions.

Japanese Salad Dressing

8 tablespoons vinegar
8 tablespoons soy sauce
1½ cups pure vegetable
   oil
½ lemon, juice
2 ounces celery juice
2 tablespoons salt
1 teaspoon pepper

Blend all ingredients together thoroughly. Serve over crisp lettuce, red cabbage and tomato. Makes 8 portions.

LA ROTISSERIE
Dearborn, Michigan • illustration by Robert Boston

The main dining room in the glittering new Hyatt Regency hotel is popular with gourmets for its imaginative fine food and excellent service. Lunch and dinner served every weekday; Sunday brunch from 10:30 a.m. to 2:30 p.m. Closed on Sunday evening. Reservations necessary for dining room and overnight accommodations. The hotel complex is located at the northwest corner of Michigan Avenue and the Southfield Freeway, south of the Fairlane Town Center. Take the Ford Road or Michigan Avenue exit from Southfield Freeway (State Highway 39).

Shrimp Szechuan

1 pound fresh raw
   shrimp, peeled
1 egg white
1 teaspoon white wine
1 teaspoon salt
1 tablespoon cornstarch
4 cups peanut oil, for
   deep frying
2 tablespoons chopped
   green onion
1 tablespoon chopped
   fresh ginger
3 tablespoons clear
   chicken stock
½ teaspoon salt
2 teaspoons cornstarch
1 tablespoon Tabasco
   sauce
1 teaspoon sesame oil

Rinse and dry shrimp, then marinate in mixture of egg white, wine, salt and cornstarch for at least 30 minutes. Deep-fry shrimp in hot oil until shrimp turn white and are about 90 per cent done. Remove shrimp and drain oil. Put 2 tablespoons of the oil in a skillet or wok and quickly stir-fry green onion and chopped ginger. Add soup stock, salt and cornstarch, stirring while pouring. Then add shrimp, and Tabasco sauce and sesame oil. Pour on a hot plate and serve with rice. Makes 4 portions.

ALIETTE'S BAKERY
Detroit, Michigan • illustration by Lin Ervine

Aliette Lanneluc-Sanson presides over this superb French bakery and small bistro. Lunch and dinner are served every day except Sunday and Monday. Reservations necessary. Advance orders for baked goods are recommended. Almost in the shadow of the Ambassador Bridge to Canada, it is just off the Porter Street exits of I-75 and I-96 at Porter and 24th Streets.

Blanquette de Veau

Sauté 6 cups bite-size veal (about 3 pounds) in 2 tablespoons of butter until meat is slightly brown. Add 1 cup of peeled small white onions and 1 pound of mushroom caps. Season with a small pinch thyme, 1 small bay leaf, dash of nutmeg, pinch of fresh parsley and salt and pepper, to taste. Cover pan and let cook gently for 45 minutes, then add ½ cup dry white wine and cook at slow boil for 15 minutes longer. Dissolve 1 tablespoon rice flour in 1 cup heavy cream and add to veal, stirring constantly. Cook 5 minutes more, stirring with care so as not to crush the meat. Serve with boiled potatoes, hot rice or noodles. Makes 6 servings.

LA FONTAINE
Detroit, Michigan • illustration by Linda Meek

La Fontaine is a delightful French restaurant in Detroit's newest riverfront jewel, the Detroit Plaza Hotel, in the heart of Renaissance Center. It is one of more than a dozen restaurants in this ultra-modern hotel designed by architect John Portman and operated by Western International Hotels. It is open for lunch Monday through Friday and dinner Monday through Saturday. Closed Sunday and major holidays. Reservations necessary. From I-75 stay on X-Way to Jefferson Avenue, turn left at Renaissance Center.

Lobster Flambé

2 large African lobster
   tails (about 1 pound)
4 tablespoons butter
½ to 1 teaspoon sweet
   basil

Salt and pepper
1 ounce Pernod (anise-
   flavored liqueur)
1 ounce white wine
2 ounces heavy cream

Cut lobster tails in bite-size pieces. Melt butter in saucepan over moderate heat. Add lobster and sprinkle in basil as the lobster sautés. Sprinkle with salt and pepper. Turn lobster frequently until a brownish residue forms on bottom of pan. (Cooking time, 10 to 15 minutes.) Pour Pernod and wine over lobster, coating all pieces. Handle carefully, a flame may arise. Remove lobster from pan and keep warm. Add cream to pan, turning and raising brown residue from bottom of pan. Return lobster to pan. As the cream thickens, it will put light glaze on lobster. Can be served as an appetizer or entree. As an entree, serve with rice pilaf, green vegetable and ½ broiled tomato. Serves 2.

Le Supreme de Volaille Divan
(Chicken Breasts with Vegetables)

6 chicken breasts, boned
   and split (marinated in
   white wine and thyme)
Seasoned flour
4 ounces clarified butter
3 ounces white wine
6 eggplant slices,
   sautéed in butter

8 ounces cooked,
   buttered noodles
2 cups brown chicken
   sauce with
   mushrooms
6 peach halves filled with
   cranberry sauce
Chopped parsley

Pat chicken breasts dry and dredge in seasoned flour. Heat butter in large skillet, add chicken and sauté until golden brown on both sides. Pour in wine and simmer gently. To serve, arrange eggplant slices in casserole dish, top each with chicken and pour sauce over the top. Arrange noodles around chicken, garnish with peach halves and sprinkle chopped parsley over chicken. Serves 6.

THE MONEY TREE
Detroit, Michigan • illustration by Susan Naughton

Specializing in French provincial cookery, this delightful restaurant is in downtown Detroit, 333 West Fort Street at Washington Boulevard. Lunch, Monday through Friday; dinner, Tuesday through Saturday. Reservations required. Helen Baumgartner is the resident pastry chef.

Almond Pound Cake

Nut Pastry, prepared in
   advance (below)
½ pound almond paste
½ pound sugar
½ pound butter

5 eggs
2 teaspoons vanilla
6 ounces sifted cake
   flour

Mix almond paste and sugar until smooth and creamy. Add butter; cream until smooth. Add eggs, one at a time, beating after each addition. Add vanilla and cake flour and blend well. Pour into nut pastry torte shells and bake at 350° 45 to 60 minutes or until done. Turn out of pans, decorate with nuts and top with glaze.

Nut Pastry

2½ cups flour	2 egg yolks
½ cup sugar	2½ cups finely ground
½ pound butter	walnuts

Combine flour and sugar on board. Chop butter into it until mixture is crumbly. Make a well in center and drop in egg yolks. Sprinkle with ground walnuts and work together with a pallet knife until well blended. Finish kneading into a ball by hand, wrap and chill 30 minutes. Roll out between sheets of waxed paper. Line 2 9-inch torte pans (with removable bases) with a thin layer of the pastry.

Glaze

¾ cup sugar	⅓ cup heavy cream,
2 tablespoons corn syrup	scalded
6 tablespoons butter	

Place sugar and corn syrup in saucepan and cook until carmelized to a golden brown. Stir in butter, then add scalded cream and blend well. Let glaze drip down sides of cakes and serve warm with whipped cream.

PONTCHARTRAIN WINE CELLARS
Detroit, Michigan • illustration by Larry McManus

A bit of France transplanted to downtown Detroit, this delightful bistro is noted for its fine food, excellent wine cellar and invention of Cold Duck. Joe Beyer is the genial host and owner. Lunch and dinner served daily; reservations necessary. Closed

Sundays, holidays and the first two weeks in July, it is at 234 West Larned.

Chicken Gabrielle

3 pounds cooked chicken, diced	1 teaspoon curry powder
	4 drops Tabasco sauce
1 pound cooked broccoli or asparagus spears	4 tablespoons chopped pimento
3 cups cream of mushroom soup	4 tablespoons grated Parmesan cheese
1 cup cream	Paprika

Place broccoli or asparagus in greased shallow baking dish. Arrange chicken over. Combine soup, cream, curry powder and Tabasco. Heat, stirring constantly, until smooth. Add pimento. Pour sauce over chicken and sprinkle with cheese and paprika. Bake for 15 minutes at 400°. Serves 8.

Choucroute Garnie

Line a big kettle with 10 slices of bacon. Wash 6 cups of sauerkraut and place in kettle. Add 6 ¾-inch thick pork chops and season with 2 teaspoons pepper and 3 tablespoons dill. Add just enough dry white wine to cover the ingredients (about 2 quarts). Put a lid on the kettle and simmer gently for 4 hours. Then add 6 knackwurst, and cook for 15-20 minutes longer. Meanwhile, boil 6 unpeeled potatoes. Arrange sauerkraut in the center of a large platter, surrounded by pork chops and sausages. Serve with peeled boiled potatoes. This makes a good buffet dish to prepare the day before and reheat. Serves 6.

ROWE INN
Ellsworth, Michigan • illustration by Randall McKissick

Two former teachers, Arlene and Wes Westhoven, operate this charming Ellsworth restaurant. The knotty-pine paneled dining room has fresh flowers, fat candles, graceful tulip-shaped goblets and cone-folded yellow napkins on Dutch blue covered tables. Open for dinner every day; closed on Monday from the first of September through June. The Inn is 35 miles north of Traverse City and a mile east of Ellsworth on County Road 48. Reservations necessary.

Shrimp Moska

36 jumbo shrimp in the shell	¼ teaspoon pepper, freshly ground
⅓ cup olive oil	¼ teaspoon salt
6 garlic cloves, finely chopped	3 whole bay leaves
	1½ cups dry white wine
1 teaspoon ground oregano	3 cups cooked wild and brown rice, combined
1 tablespoon dried rosemary leaves	Chopped parsley
	Lemon wedges

At low heat warm olive oil in a frying pan that is large enough to hold the shrimp without stacking them. Add garlic and sauté gently for a moment. Place shrimp in the pan and sprinkle with herbs and spices. Turn shrimp to distribute the seasonings evenly. Sauté gently for 5 minutes. Add enough white wine to cover shrimp. Turn up to heat and cook until wine and olive oil are reduced to a syrup. Remove bay leaves. Arrange shrimp (still in the shell) in individual bowls over rice. Sprinkle parsley over shrimp and pour cooking liquid over each portion. Garnish with lemon wedges and serve with finger bowls. Makes 6 portions.

GIBBS COUNTRY HOUSE
Ludington, Michigan • illustration by Randall McKissick

Located on U.S. Highways 10 and 31 between Ludington and Scottville on Michigan's western shore, this restaurant prides itself on homemade breads, desserts and ice cream. Owner Harold Gibbs offers guests an "all you can eat" challenge from his buffet and "help yourself" dessert table. Lunch and dinner daily; open until all guests are served. Closed from January 1 to April 4.

Health Bread

Heat together to melt shortening: 1½ cups milk, ¼ cup shortening and 1½ teaspoons salt. When shortening has melted, add 1½ cups cold water. Let cool until warm. Then add 2 cakes compressed yeast or equivalent of dry yeast and ⅓ cup brown sugar or molasses. Stir the following amounts of flour into the first mixture: ½ cup wheat germ, ½ cup finely

ground whole wheat, 2 cups flaked whole wheat and 5 cups white flour. Dough should be soft and elastic. Let rise until double in bulk, then divide dough into 2 portions and shape each into a loaf, kneading gently. Place in buttered bread pans. Butter tops of loaves and let rise until just about top of breadpan. Bake at 350° for about 45 minutes. Makes 2 loaves. *(If flaked whole wheat is not available, you may substitute rolled oats or regular whole wheat flour, or order the flaked whole wheat from: The Fruit Cellar, 23822 Ford Road, Dearborn Heights, Michigan 48127.)*

GRAND HOTEL
Mackinac Island, Michigan • illustration by Gilbert DiCicco

On a bluff overlooking the Straits of Mackinac and surrounded by 500 acres of beautifully landscaped grounds, the resort has the world's largest summer hotel. Completed in 1887, the hotel is open from mid-May to mid-October. Breakfast, lunch and dinner served every day. Reservations required for meals and overnight accommodations. There are full recreation facilities for guests. No cars are allowed on the island. Guests arrive by private boat or by ferry from Mackinaw City or St. Ignace, Michigan, and are transported from the dock to the hotel by horsedrawn carriages.

Indian Corn Soup

Sauté 2 stalks chopped celery and 1 small chopped onion in ⅓ cup butter over low heat until straw colored. Then mix in 3 tablespoons flour with a little water and stir until thickened. Add 4 cups half and half and cook until mixture thickens slightly. Heat 4 cups cream style corn and add to cream mixture and bring to boiling point. Season with 1 teaspoon salt and ½ teaspoon pepper. Sprinkle with a little chopped parsley and serve piping hot. Makes 6 portions.

Chicken Delmar

Dip 6 chicken legs and thighs in ½ cup melted butter and then roll in 1 cup cracker crumbs. Place on a rack in a roast pan and bake at 450° for 20 minutes. Reduce heat to 275° and bake until very tender, about 1½ hours. Serve with 2 cups gravy made from chicken stock and thickened with flour and cream. Add small amount of sage and poultry seasoning to gravy. Serves 6.

FRANKY'S RESTAURANT

Niles, Michigan • illustration by Max Altekruse

Frank Frucci, Jr., is the owner of this antique-filled restaurant at 1031 Lake Street in Niles. Lunch and dinner are served every day except Tuesday. Sunday brunch served at 11 a.m. The gift shop, next to the restaurant, is in a converted caboose. It is 5 blocks east of State Highway 51.

Veal Scaloppine

12 2-ounce pieces of veal cutlet	4 cups beef bouillon
½ cup flour	2 cups sliced, cooked mushrooms
3 tablespoons butter	6 ounces dry sherry
8 slices of onion	Salt, pepper, oregano
8 thick tomato slices	and garlic powder, to
8 large pieces of green pepper, cooked	taste

Flatten veal medallions very thin. Dredge in flour and brown in butter. Remove veal. In the same pan, sauté onion, tomato slices and green pepper. Add bouillon. Let simmer. Add mushrooms, sherry and seasonings. Simmer for about 5 minutes. Put meat on plates and cover with sauce. Makes 4 servings.

AH WOK RESTAURANT

Novi, Michigan • illustration by Max Altekruse

Fine Chinese food is served in a pleasant dining room in this eating place in a suburb of Detroit. At 41563 West Ten Mile Road, it is two miles southeast of I-96. Take Novi Road exit. Lunch and dinner served every day except Monday. Reservations necessary.

Velvet Chicken

Take 3 whole boned chicken breasts and slice into strips about ⅙ of an inch thick. Mix chicken with 1 teaspoon cornstarch, ½ teaspoon salt, ¼ teaspoon white pepper, 1 teaspoon soy sauce and 2 tablespoons vegetable oil. Let mixture stand. Take a 4-ounce can of white button mushrooms and heat with a sauce made of a combination of 2 teaspoons cornstarch and ½ teaspoon salt dissolved in ¼ cup mushroom liquid. Take a slice of fresh ginger root and a garlic clove and chop very fine and fry in 2 tablespoons of vegetable oil in a wok or heavy skillet. Add chicken mixture and fry over hot fire for about

30 seconds, pour in hot mushroom mixture and continue cooking until chicken turns white all over and is just done. Serve hot and quickly — care must be taken not to overcook chicken. Serve over hot rice. Serves 4.

HOTEL MAYFLOWER AND MOTOR INN
Plymouth, Michigan • illustration by Max Altekruse

"Good food and hospitality" is the way Ralph G. Lorenz, owner of this 50-year-old inn, describes his dining rooms. In line with the Early American atmosphere, many of the foods stem from historical backgrounds. The Mayflower Room is open for breakfast, lunch and dinner year round. The London Pub has lunch, cocktails and nightly entertainment and the Steak-House Galley steaks and scrod. Overnight accommodations. Reservations necessary. Address is 827 West Ann Arbor Trail.

Mayflower Indian Pudding

3 cups milk	½ teaspoon ground
⅓ cup molasses	ginger
⅓ cup yellow cornmeal	½ teaspoon ground
2 tablespoons butter	cinnamon
1 egg, beaten	¼ teaspoon salt
¼ cup sugar	

Combine milk and molasses in saucepan and stir in cornmeal. Cook and stir over medium heat about 10 minutes or until thick. Remove from heat and stir in butter. Beat egg with sugar, spices and salt. Gradually stir in cornmeal mixture. Turn into buttered 6-cup baking dish. Bake at 300° about 1½ hours. Serve hot with small scoop vanilla ice cream.

Spiced Carrots

2 pounds carrots	1 cup sugar
1 quart white vinegar	1 teaspoon Maggi
½ cup mixed pickling spices	

Scrape and cut carrots into chunks or slices. Cook in salted water until just tender. Drain. Let cool. Bring vinegar, spices, sugar and Maggi to boiling. Pour over carrots and let stand overnight. May be packed in small jars and refrigerated. Good with lamb or veal.

THE RIVER CRAB
St. Clair, Michigan • illustration by J. M. Whittlesey

Diners arrive by boat or car at this lively and colorful riverside establishment on the St. Clair River. The restaurant is owned by Chuck Muer. Lunch and dinner served daily; overnight accommodations; reservations advisable. It is two miles north of the city of St. Clair on the River Road.

Charley's Chowder

In a large soup pot sauté 3 crushed cloves of garlic in 4 tablespoons of olive oil until golden, taking care not to burn. Remove garlic. Add 1 finely chopped onion and sauté for two minutes. Add a pinch each of basil, oregano and thyme and cook for another minute. Add 3 stalks of celery finely chopped and cook until translucent. Add 6 ounces stewed tomatoes, chopped very fine, and cook for about 20-25 minutes, stirring to prevent sticking. Add 3 quarts of water, 1 pound boneless fish (pollack or turbot) and 2 ounces clam base and cook for an additional 15 minutes, uncovered at full heat. (If clam base is not available substitute 3 quarts clam juice and omit water.) Salt to taste, cover the pot and cook at low heat for another 20 minutes. Stir often by whipping to break up the fish and blend the flavors. Add freshly chopped parsley. Makes 8-10 generous servings.

SHIELD'S

Traverse City, Michigan • illustration by Susan Naughton

Arne and Katie Shield are the owners, as well as the genial hosts, at this popular family restaurant in a 100-year-old building at 2900 Munson Avenue (U.S. Highway 31) in Traverse City. The menu is varied with special emphasis on fresh seafood. Shield's is famous for dessert carts which are rolled to diners' tables filled with a dazzling array of homemade pies, cakes and pastries. Open for lunch and dinner every day except December 24 and 25. Reservations advisable.

Black Forest Torte

Place the following in a mixing bowl: 1¾ cups flour, 1¾ cups sugar, 1¼ teaspoons soda, 1 teaspoon salt, ¼ teaspoon baking powder, ⅔ cup chiffon-type soft margarine (no substitutes), 4 ounces melted and cooled unsweetened chocolate, 1 teaspoon vanilla and 1¼ cups of water. Beat together at medium speed for 4-5 minutes. Add 3 whole eggs and beat for 2 minutes. Pour batter into 4 buttered 9-inch cake pans, bake in 350° oven for 15-18 minutes. Cool before filling. Spread first layer with half of chocolate filling (below), add the second layer and cover with half of the cream filling (below). Repeat, having cream filling on top. Chill cake until firm before serving.

Chocolate Filling

Melt 6 ounces German's sweet chocolate, let cool. Blend in ¾ cup chiffon-type margarine and ½ cup chopped, toasted almonds.

Cream Filling

Beat 2 cups whipping cream with 1 tablespoon sugar and 1 teaspoon vanilla. Beat until stiff.

UNDER THE WILLOW

Traverse City, Michigan • illustration by James Stocker

This delightful restaurant is part of Logan's Landing,

a unique tourist attraction three miles south of Traverse City off U.S. Highway 31. The Landing rests on the east and west banks of the Boardman River joined by a beautiful covered bridge. The dining room is right on the river, where mute swans, ducks and wild fowl often are in view of diners. Lunch and dinner served daily.

Oriental Steak

1½ pounds flank or round steak	1 teaspoon Adolph's meat tenderizer
2 green peppers	1 ounce dry sherry
2 large onions	Salt and pepper, to taste
4 tablespoons salad oil (approximately)	2 tablespoons soy sauce
	2 cups hot buttered rice
	1 pound cherry tomatoes

Cut steak into pieces 1 by 2 inches. Cut onions and green peppers in approximately the same size pieces. Brown steak in just enough oil to cover the skillet. Add soy sauce and tenderizer. Cook to medium rare. Add sherry, cook to medium. In another pan lightly sauté onions and green peppers in oil for 1 minute. Season with salt, pepper and additional soy sauce, to taste. Arrange sautéed vegetables over portions of hot rice, then top with meat. Garnish plates with raw cherry tomatoes. Makes 6 servings.

COUNTRY INN

Utica, Michigan • illustration by George C. Warner

Paintings by local artists decorate the walls of this cheery restaurant housed in a historic old home in Utica, 13 miles northeast of Detroit. It is open every weekday for lunch and dinner; the only weekend meal, Sunday dinner, is served from 2 to 8 p.m. Reservations advisable. It is at 45199 Cass Avenue, a block north of Hall Road (State Highway 59). The owner-manager is Joseph V. Fratarcangeli.

Veal Parmesan

8 2-ounce veal cutlets
⅓ cup oil
Egg mixture (below)
Crumb mixture (below)
8 slices Mozzarella
   cheese

1½ cups rich tomato
   sauce
4 tablespoons grated
   Parmesan cheese

Dip cutlets into egg mixture and then dredge in crumb mixture. Fry in skillet in 325° oil until golden brown. Place cutlets on oven-proof plates and cover each with a slice of cheese, then broil until cheese bubbles. Top with hot tomato sauce and sprinkle with grated Parmesan cheese. Serves 4.

Egg mixture

Beat together 2 eggs, ¼ teaspoon salt, ¼ teaspoon pepper, 2 tablespoons grated Parmesan cheese and 1 clove crushed garlic.

Crumb mixture

Combine 2 cups bread crumbs with ¼ teaspoon salt, ¼ teaspoon pepper, 1 clove crushed garlic and 4 tablespoons grated Parmesan cheese.

HAAB'S RESTAURANT
Ypsilanti, Michigan • illustration by Robert Boston

Since 1934 when it was founded by Otto and Oscar Haab, this homey restaurant has been an area tradition with a reputation for serving only prime grade beef and the freshest ingredients in other menu items. The brothers are now retired but their ironclad rules on quality are carried on by the new owners Mike Kabat and Harvey Glaze. A peek into the modern kitchen reveals many busy hands baking bread, whipping up mayonnaise, even preparing homemade noodles. Open for lunch and dinner every day. The address is 18 West Michigan Avenue on U.S. 12 off I-94.

Prime Steak London Broil Marinade

6 boneless prime top
   sirloin steaks
1 cup red wine
⅓ cup vinegar
½ cup salad oil
¼ teaspoon sweet basil
¼ teaspoon oregano

¼ teaspoon black
   pepper
2 teaspoons salt
1 small garlic clove,
   crushed
2 teaspoons chopped
   onion
1 bay leaf, broken

Have steaks cut 1 inch thick, 10 ounces each. Combine wine, vinegar, oil, basil, oregano, pepper, salt, garlic, onion, and bay leaf. Pour over steaks, cover and let stand in refrigerator 8 hours. Broil to preferred degree of doneness. Serves 6.

IRON DUKE
Duluth, Minnesota • illustration by Richard A. Young

One of the restaurants in the Spirit Mountain Recreation Area, the Iron Duke is 10 minutes west of downtown Duluth. Take Interstate 35, exit at

Boundary Avenue and proceed about a mile to the resort. Breakfast, lunch and dinner and late supper served every day. The resort offers a full recreation program year round with excellent downhill and cross-country ski facilities in the winter. There is a beautiful campground in the summer. Reservations advised for dinner during the ski season and at any time of year for overnight accommodations.

Old-Fashioned Corn Bread

4 strips thick bacon	1 teaspoon salt
1 small green pepper, diced	4 tablespoons baking powder
1 small onion, diced	3 eggs
4 cups white flour	3 cups buttermilk
2 cups corn meal	½ cup cooking oil
¼ cup sugar	

Cut bacon into small pieces and sauté in skillet. Add diced pepper and onion and sauté. Let cool slightly. In a mixing bowl combine flour, corn meal, sugar, salt and baking powder. Mix well. Beat eggs slightly and add to dry ingredients along with buttermilk and oil. Add onion and pepper mixture. Pour into greased 8x10 pan and bake 45 minutes or until done in a 375° oven.

CICERO'S

Roseville, Minnesota • illustration by Bruce Bond

The dining room is reminiscent of the 1920s and there is entertainment nightly with music from a 1928 Wurlitzer organ. The menu of Italian dishes and sandwiches is geared to the whole family. It is located in the Har Mar Mall, two miles north of I-94 at 2100 North Snelling Avenue (State Highway 51) in suburban St. Paul. Lunch and dinner served every day. Michael Belknap is the owner.

Cicero's Salad

On a bed of crisp lettuce, shred approximately 1 head of fresh iceberg lettuce which has been washed and allowed to dry. Add the following ingredients (all cut in thin julienne strips): 3 ounces white breast of turkey, 3 ounces lean smoked ham, 3 ounces lean corned beef and 3 ounces American cheese. Top with the following ingredients: 3 ounces shredded Mozzarella cheese, 2 ounces anchovies, cut in pieces, 2 quartered ripe tomatoes and 2 ounces fresh garlic croutons. Over this, pour your favorite salad dressing or the special Cicero's Italian dressing (below). Makes 4 portions.

Italian Dressing

Take 6 ounces of chilled olive or corn oil, add 2 ounces wine vinegar, 1 teaspoon fresh mashed garlic, ½ teaspoon fresh oregano, ¼ teaspoon sweet basil, ½ teaspoon salt and ½ teaspoon freshly ground pepper. Mix well and refrigerate for 24 hours before using. Mix well before each use. Makes enough dressing for 4 generous salads.

CHOUETTE

Wayzata, Minnesota • illustration by Jim Stelma

Jean Claude Tindillier, a French chef, presides over the kitchen of this fine dining spot owned by Mrs. Jolley F. White. Located across the road from Lake Minnetonka, the restaurant serves meals in four small dining rooms with the finest of silver, linens and glassware. It is more like having dinner in a private home than a restaurant. Lunch and dinner served every day, except Sunday. Reservations necessary. It is about 20 miles west of Minneapolis at 739 Lake Street in downtown Wayzata.

Salade de Canard aux Poires Fraiches

Roast a 4-pound duckling to perfection. Let cool then remove skin and bones. The meat should be slivered. Slice 3 whole Bartlett pears. Add 7 ounces very light mayonnaise to combined sliced duckling and pears, and toss lightly. Serve on bed of Boston leaf lettuce with radishes, black olives and tomato wedges. Top with blanched almonds and serve cold. Serves 6-8.

French Onion Soup

Sauté 4 cups minced onions in 1 tablespoon peanut oil and 2 tablespoons butter until onions are golden brown. Drain oil and butter, add 8 cups rich, seasoned chicken broth. Season with ¼ teaspoon white pepper. Bring to boil, then reduce heat. Simmer for 30 minutes. Add dash of port, if desired. Pour into 6-8 earthen casseroles and top each with finely sliced pieces of toasted French bread and sprinkle with 10 ounces grated Swiss cheese. Bake in 400° oven for about 25 minutes or until cheese is melted and the top is golden brown. Serves 6-8.

COPPER HEARTH DINING ROOM
North Platte, Nebraska • illustration by George Samerjan

A fine Austrian chef, Hans Pircher, presides over the kitchen that is open daily from 6 a.m. to 10 p.m. Each month the menu features a different selection of gourmet specialties. It is in a Holiday Inn at the junction of U.S. 83 and I-80. The inn offers overnight accommodations, swimming pool, saunas and a putting green. Reservations suggested.

Poulet Basquaise

1 3-pound chicken, quartered	1 teaspoon salt
2 tablespoons butter	½ teaspoon pepper

½ cup sliced onion	1 tomato, diced, 1 clove
1 medium green pepper, sliced	garlic and 1 bay leaf
½ cup mushrooms, quartered	½ cup dry white wine
	½ cup beef stock

Brown chicken quarters on all sides in enough butter to cover the bottom of a skillet. Sprinkle chicken with salt and pepper and put it in a deep casserole. In the fat in which the chicken was browned, stir together vegetables, garlic clove and bay leaf. Brown vegetables until a light color. Arrange around chicken pieces in casserole. Pour white wine in skillet and add beef stock, bring to a boil, then pour over chicken. Cover casserole and bake in a 350° oven for about 40 minutes, or until chicken is tender. Serve over hot buttered rice or rice pilaf.

THE FRENCH CAFE
Omaha, Nebraska • illustration by Allen Tubach

Located in the old market area of downtown Omaha at 1017 Howard, this restaurant offers luncheon and by-reservation-only dinners. Lunch is served Monday through Friday 11:30 a.m. to 2 p.m.; dinner Monday through Saturday from 6 p.m. Michael Harrison is the owner. Closed Sunday.

Blanquette of Veal

2¼ pounds shoulder or breast of veal	4 carrots, peeled and quartered
Water	2 tablespoons flour
1 large onion	2 tablespoons butter
2 stalks parsley	2 large egg yolks
6 peppercorns	½ cup whipping cream
2 teaspoons salt	½ pound small mushroom caps, sautéed in butter
1 clove garlic	
12 small white onions, peeled	

Cut meat into 2-inch pieces and parboil 5 minutes in a saucepan in water to cover. Drain. Add the large onion, parsley, peppercorns, salt and garlic, with water to cover (about 4 cups). Bring to boiling point, reduce heat, and simmer 1½ hours or until veal is tender. Add small onions and carrots 30 minutes before cooking time is up. Using a perforated spoon, transfer meat, carrots and onions to a serving dish and keep hot. Strain stock and reduce to about two-thirds. Blend the flour with the butter, add to the broth, bring to a boiling point and cook 1 minute. Beat egg yolks lightly with cream and stir into the broth. Stir and heat until sauce thickens. (Do not boil.) Adjust seasonings. Pour over the meat, carrots, and onions. Garnish with mushroom caps. Serve with rice or boiled potatoes. Makes 6 servings.

TAIL OF THE WHALE
Fargo, North Dakota • illustration by Bruce Bond

This fine restaurant is in the Fargo Biltmore Motor Hotel at 3700 Main Avenue (U.S. 10) a half block west of I-29. Open daily for breakfast, lunch and dinner. Reservations advisable for dinner and for overnight accomodations. Edward Rafferty is the manager.

Whole Dover Sole

Place 4 frozen whole Dover sole in warm water just long enough to thaw through skin. Remove from water. Cut through skin only just above the tail, and start to peel skin from tail toward head in a steady motion. Do this to both sides of fish. After removing skin, remove head and tail with poultry scissors. Fish should be thawed at this time. Place sole in 4 beaten eggs, roll in 1 cup of flour seasoned with white pepper and salt and dip again in egg. Brown fish lightly on both sides in a greased frying pan. Place in baking dish and bake at 425°, about 15-20 minutes. Remove sole and place on serving platter. With sharp

knife cut down the center of the fish. With flat spatula fold back each side of incision and gently pull out bone. Replace each side to give appearance of whole sole. Sprinkle with fresh lemon juice and garnish with slivered almonds. Serves 4.

CHESTER'S ROAD HOUSE
Cincinnati, Ohio • illustration by Lin Ervine

Michael and Lee Comisar are the owners of this beautiful restaurant at 9678 Montgomery Road. From I-75 take I-275 (East) to the Montgomery Road exit. Proceed south three miles to the restaurant. A garden-like atmosphere dominates the two plant-filled dining rooms, one of which is under a glass roof. Dinner served every day except Christmas Eve, Christmas and Thanksgiving Day.

Mushrooms Road House

1 pound fresh mushrooms	5 ounces garlic butter (below)
3 tablespoons oil	¼ cup chopped parsley
	Salt and pepper, to taste

Sauté whole mushrooms in hot oil until they are slightly brown. Remove excess oil. Add garlic butter and seasonings, and heat. Serve when the butter begins to foam. Add chopped parsley just before serving.

Chester's Garlic Butter

½ pound butter (unsalted)	1 tablespoon chopped parsley
2 teaspoons fresh chopped garlic	1 teaspoon chopped shallots

Let butter soften. Add garlic, chopped parsley and chopped shallots. Mix well. Serves 3.

AU PROVENCE
Cleveland Heights, Ohio • illustration by Don Odle

Dr. Thomas Wykoff, the owner, produces his own wines in the cellar of the restaurant and these vintages accompany the French and New Orleans Creole dishes served in the small, country-French dining room. Dinner served Monday through Thursday 6 p.m. to 10 p.m.; Friday 6 to midnight (no reservations accepted). Saturday seatings are at 6:30 p.m. and 9:15 p.m., by reservation only. The address is 2195 Lee Road, Cleveland Heights.

Raisin Sauce au Provence

15 ounces seedless raisins
2 tablespoons brown sugar
2 teaspoons ground cinnamon
1 teaspoon ground ginger

½ pound butter, melted
⅓ cup Grand Marnier (or other orange-flavored liqueur)
⅓ cup warm water

In a blender or Cuisinart, combine sugar, spices, melted butter and Grand Marnier. While the ingredients are blending, place raisins in a strainer and immerse in a pot filled with hot tap water until raisins are tender. Add raisins to blender and puree well. As mixture thickens, add a little of the warm water to attain a pouring consistency. Keep warm. Serve warm over acorn squash, or at room temperature on cheesecake. Makes 2 to 3 cups of sauce. Store in refrigerator.

BLACK ANGUS STEAK HOUSE
Kalida, Ohio • illustration by William Noonan

In 1936 this restaurant started out as a small family operation. Today it is still run by the Kuhlman family,

but it has nine dining rooms and seats over 600 patrons. Breakfast, lunch and dinner served daily; reservations advisable. The address is 104 Main Street in downtown Kalida, at the junction of State Highways 114, 115 and U.S. 224.

Browned Steak with Tomato Sauce

1½ pounds round steak, 1½ inches thick
4 tablespoons flour
4 tablespoons oil
½ cup chopped onions
2 tablespoons chopped parsley

1 tablespoon salt
¼ teaspoon pepper
2 bay leaves
1½ cups tomato sauce
1 cup water
2 tablespoons brown sugar

Roll steak in flour, coating evenly on both sides. Add oil to a heavy skillet, heat, then brown steak well on both sides. Remove from pan and keep warm. Combine remaining ingredients, bring to a boil and pour over browned steak. Reduce heat and simmer covered for 1½ hours. Serves 6.

BUCKINGHAM INN
Lima, Ohio • illustration by Marcus Hamilton

The atmosphere is Old-English here but the menu travels the world. George Kookootsedes and John Giokaris are the owners of this establishment located just outside the western city limits of Lima at 1800 Elida Road (State Highway 309). Lunch and dinner served daily; reservations necessary. Closed holidays.

Chicken Grand Marnier

4 chicken breasts, split
1½ cups flour
1 teaspoon ginger

Salt and pepper, to taste
1½ sticks butter
3 cups water

Combine flour, ginger, salt and pepper. Shake chicken in bag with seasoned flour. Brown chicken in

½ stick butter over brisk heat. Place in casserole, add water and remaining butter. Bake 30 minutes in a 375° oven, basting frequently. Place in a chafing dish and cover with sauce (below).

Sauce

Sauté 2 tablespoons minced white onion in 2 teaspoons butter. Drain No. 303 size can apricot halves, retaining juice. Measure apricot juice and add enough chicken stock to make 2 cups. Blend 2 tablespoons cornstarch moistened with water into the apricot juice mixture, then combine with sautéed onions. Bring to a boil, stirring constantly. Add apricots. Pour over chicken. Warm and ignite ¼ cup Grand Marnier and pour over chicken. Serve with hot rice. Makes 8 portions.

HOMESTEAD INN
Milan, Ohio • illustration by Gilbert DiCicco

Mr. and Mrs. J. P. Henry, who own and operate this charming country inn, also raise their own cattle. In the surrounding pastures guests may see their "steaks on the hoof." The dining room is open every day from 7 a.m. to 9 p.m.; closed most major holidays. Overnight accommodations and recreation facilities. Take Exit 7 from the Ohio Turnpike; the inn is a quarter mile south on U.S. 250.

Swiss Steak

2 pounds round steak, pounded	½ cup diced onion
1 cup flour	¼ cup diced green pepper
½ teaspoon salt	3 tablespoons flour
⅛ teaspoon pepper	⅓ cup tomato juice
2 tablespoons oil	2 cups water
½ cup chopped celery	

Mix flour, salt and pepper. Dredge meat in flour mixture. Brown in oil. Remove meat to a casserole. Sauté celery, onion and green pepper in the skillet from which the meat has been removed. Make a gravy by adding flour, water and tomato juice to the vegetables. Pour over meat and bake in 375° oven for 1½ hours. Serves 6.

Corning Brine for Beef Brisket

Whole fresh brisket of beef	¾ pound sugar
1 gallon water	2¼ pounds salt
2 ounces saltpeter	¼ cup mixed pickling spices

Boil the water, then add saltpeter, sugar, salt and spices. Cool, then add meat. Top meat with a heavy plate to keep it covered with brine. Marinate for 3 weeks in a cool place. Remove, rinse off meat and cover with cold water; add 1 teaspoon mixed pickling spices. Bring to a boil and simmer until fork tender, about 3 hours. Serve hot or cold, sliced thin.

PIONEER MILL
Tiffin, Ohio • illustration by Frank Webb

The building housing this fine restaurant was originally an old flour mill established on the Sandusky River in 1822. Its turbines still operate and provide electricity. Lunch and dinner served every day. The address is 255 Riverside Drive.

Onion Soup

4 large Spanish onions	4 beef bouillon cubes
½ cup olive oil	6 cups croutons (below)
4 quarts rich beef stock	3 ounces Swiss cheese, per serving
2 cups burgundy	
½ cup Kitchen Quick (for color and flavor)	

Slice onions and sauté in olive oil until tender. Bring beef stock to boil, add sautéed onions, wine, Kitchen Quick and bouillon cubes. Cook over low heat for 2 hours.

Croutons

Take 6 cups cubed bread and sprinkle Parmesan cheese over bread cubes; add garlic butter with butter brush. Sprinkle paprika over bread cubes. Put on a tray in 350° oven; bake until browned. Dip soup into crocks, add croutons. Add 3 ounces grated Swiss cheese to each crock. Bake crocks in preheated 400° oven for 10 minutes.

CAP'T BILLY'S WHIZZ BANG
Toledo, Ohio • illustration by Richard A. Young

In business for five years, this light-hearted restaurant recently expanded to double its size. There is a limited — and amusing — menu and it is a popular family eating place. Lunch is served Monday through Friday; dinner served Monday

through Saturday. Closed on Sunday. The address is 2111 Mellwood Street in Toledo. From I-475 take either Secor Road or Jackman Road north to Laskey; it is at the corner of Laskey and Mellwood.

Jambalaya

6 slices bacon, chopped and fried	A pinch each of cayenne, cloves
1 onion, diced	1 tablespoon flour
1 green pepper, diced	1 No. 2½ can of tomatoes, chopped
2 tablespoons chopped parsley	1 pound cleaned raw shrimp
½ teaspoon black pepper	6 boneless chicken breasts, broiled
¼ teaspoon thyme and nutmeg	3 cups cooked rice

Remove bacon pieces from pan and in bacon fat sauté onion and green pepper. Add all of the seasonings and sauté until onion and green pepper are tender. Slowly add flour and stir mixture until the flour is well blended. Add tomatoes, let simmer a few minutes. Add shrimp and simmer until the shrimp turn pink. Place broiled chicken breasts on hot rice. Ladle shrimp mixture over them and top with bacon pieces. Serves 6.

OLD MARKET HOUSE INN
Zanesville, Ohio • illustration by Clarence Kincaid

Located directly across the street from where the town's old produce market once stood, this inn is a charming re-creation of the inns of yesterday. There are deep brown oak cathedral ceilings, stained glass windows and an impressive collection of paintings by the artist Leslie Cope. Dinner served every day except Sunday. From I-70 going west, take Downtown Exit U.S. 40 to Market Street. The restaurant is at 424 Market Street. James Adornetto is the owner-manager.

Mocha Torte

35 large marshmallows
¾ cup double strength
   instant coffee
½ pint whipping cream,
   whipped

2 3-ounce packages lady
   fingers
½ cup sliced, toasted
   almonds

Melt marshmallows in coffee over low heat. Cool. Combine whipped cream and marshmallow mixture. Split lady fingers and line a 9-inch spring form pan with them. Pour in half of filling mixture. Sprinkle with toasted almonds. Add another layer of split lady fingers, then rest of filling. Chill for several hours or overnight. Serves 10-12.

CHUTE ROOSTERS

Hill City, South Dakota • illustration by J. W. Kelly, Jr.

Bette Matkins and son, Marvin, converted an 1886 barn into a charming restaurant which specializes in western foods. The restaurant is dedicated to cowboys, past and present (the term "chute roosters" is cowboy slang for a rodeo wise-guy who roosts on the chutes and tells everyone how to handle the horses). It is on U.S. Highway 385 on the east side of Hill City en route to Mt. Rushmore which is 26 miles south of Rapid City. Dinner only every day 4 p.m. to 2 a.m. A special chuck wagon dinner offered on Sunday and summer evenings. Headquarters for winter sports; adjacent lodging.

Gringo Cabbage

Coarsely chop 1 medium head of cabbage. Place in pot; sprinkle with 1 teaspoon salt. Cover with boiling water; boil 7 minutes. Drain. Place ½ of the boiled cabbage in a buttered rectangular baking dish. Pour ½ cup white sauce (below) over cabbage. Sprinkle with ½ cup Parmesan cheese and ½ cup buttered cracker crumbs. Layer remaining cabbage over

mixture. Pour white sauce over cabbage. Sprinkle with ½ cup Parmesan cheese and ½ cup buttered cracker crumbs. Bake in 350° oven for 30 minutes. Cut in 3-inch squares for serving. Serves 6.

White Sauce

⅓ cup butter or
   margarine
3 tablespoons flour
1½ cups milk

½ teaspoon salt
⅛ teaspoon cayenne
   pepper

Melt butter in a skillet; add flour. Slowly add milk. Cook and stir until thick. Add salt and pepper.

SIMON HOUSE

Glendale, Wisconsin • illustration by Bruce Bond

William Everding is the owner-manager of this handsome restaurant about 10 miles north of Milwaukee, just off I-43. Lunch and dinner are served daily; the restaurant is closed most holidays. In the summer months there is outdoor dining in the courtyard. Reservations necessary. The address is 400 West Silver Spring Drive.

Baked Shrimp à la Maurice

28 large raw, cleaned
   shrimp
¼ pound butter
3 tablespoons parsley,
   chopped

2 ounces soy sauce
1 teaspoon garlic salt
1 pound sliced bacon
2 cups cooked wild rice

Place butter, parsley, soy sauce and garlic salt in a mixing bowl. Whip for approximately 3 minutes. Butterfly the shrimp, being careful not to cut through. Place a little garlic butter in the wedge of the shrimp and wrap each with 1 strip of bacon. Broil until brown. Then bake in 400° oven for about 15 minutes. Serve on a bed of wild rice. Serves 4.

Fudge Bottom Pie

Melt 4 ounces unsweetened chocolate, add ⅓ cup of coffee, ⅓ cup of sugar and ¼ cup of milk. Stir over low heat until smooth. Pour into a chilled 10-inch graham cracker crust. Allow to cool. Add 12 ounces boiled custard and chill for 30 minutes. Top with whipped cream.

CHALET ST. MORITZ

Middleton, Wisconsin • illustration by William B. Kindred

On 20 acres of beautiful, rolling countryside, Helen and Karl Hoffman have created a chalet restaurant with a menu and decor typical of their native Switzerland. There is live entertainment, including folk dancing and singing. The Chalet is in Middleton, just a few miles west of Madison on Airport Road. Dinner is served every day except Monday. Reservations are necessary.

Cheese Casserole

Grease a casserole with butter. In a separate bowl mix 4 tablespoons flour with 2 cups of milk. Add 4 egg yolks, ¾ pound grated Cheddar cheese, and ¼ teaspoon each salt and nutmeg. Mix well and fold in 4 beaten egg whites. Pour into casserole and bake in 250°-300° oven for 30-40 minutes. Serves 4.

Cheese Potatoes

Halve lengthwise 4 cooked medium-size, peeled potatoes. Brush each with oil and place in rows on a greased baking sheet. Put into oven at 300°. When they begin to sizzle, after about 20 minutes, place a slice of sharp Cheddar cheese on top of each potato half. Return to oven and leave until the cheese melts.

MOLGAARD'S INDIAN LODGE

St. Germain, Wisconsin • illustration by Bruce Bond

Finnish and Swedish craftsmen built this log building in northern Wisconsin. One of the state's most popular resort supper clubs, it is open May 1 through October for dinner only. Closed Mondays, except Labor Day. Reservations advisable. It is on State Highway 70, 12 miles west of Eagle River and U.S. Highway 45. Gina and Joe Molgaard are the owner-managers.

Beef Burgundy

1½-2 pounds cubed stewing beef	*Salt and pepper, to taste*
2 tablespoons bacon fat, or cooking oil	*2 tablespoons flour*
1 large Bermuda onion, chopped	*2 cups beef stock or bouillon*
Generous pinch each of leaf thyme and leaf marjoram	*2 cups dry red burgundy wine*
	1 pound fresh mushrooms

Sauté beef cubes in bacon fat or oil until very brown, remove from pan. Sauté onion in the pan adding more bacon fat if necessary. Remove onions from pan and set aside. Place meat back in pan, add seasonings. Sprinkle flour over meat and stir until absorbed. Add beef stock and wine to cover meat. Simmer, covered, for 3-4 hours, adding more beef stock and wine if necessary. Add mushrooms and the sautéed onion and simmer for 30 minutes. If desired, can be thickened with cornstarch or arrowroot, dissolved in water. Serves 6.

South Central

Oysters Bienville – Anderson's, Arkansas
Rigatoni with Broccoli – Al Baker's, Missouri
Marinated Beef Loin – Cowtown Club, Kansas
Alzina's Bread Pudding – Bon Ton, Louisiana

WIEDERKEHR WEINKELLER RESTAURANT

Altus, Arkansas • illustration by Robert Handville

This charming Swiss restaurant is built around the 90-year-old wine cellars and vineyards of John Andrew Wiederkehr. Just north of the tiny village of Altus, it can be reached by taking Exit 41 from I-40 onto Route 186 and proceeding 4¼ miles south to the Weinkeller. Lunch and dinner served daily; reservations necessary for dinner. Closed most holidays. There are also free tours of the wine cellars, vineyards and the tasting bar.

Black Forest Cherry Cake

8 eggs, separated	1 teaspoon arrowroot,
1 whole egg	moistened with water
1 cup sugar	1½ pints whipping
1 level cup sponge cake	cream, whipped and
crumbs	slightly sweetened
¾ cup ground almonds	1 ounce Kirsch
½ cup flour	Chocolate shavings
2½ tablespoons cocoa	Halved cherries for top
1 cup halved sour	of cake
cherries, and juice	

Beat egg yolks, 1 whole egg with sugar and 1 tablespoon warm water. Add crumbs and ground almonds and then stiffly beaten egg whites, followed by sifted flour and cocoa. Pour batter into a greased and floured 10-inch spring form cake pan. Bake in a 375° oven for 40-45 minutes. When cold, slice cake into three separate layers. Heat cherries, cherry juice and arrowroot together until it thickens and let cool. Ice first and second layers with Kirsch-flavored whipped cream, then divide thickened cherry mixture between these two layers. Put on top layer and ice top and sides with whipped cream. Decorate the sides and a circle in the center of the cake with chocolate shavings. Pipe rosettes of whipped cream around the edge and make a circle of cherry halves around the outer edge of the cake. Chill until served. Makes 12-14 portions.

LIGHTHOUSE INN

Fort Smith, Arkansas • illustration by Richard A. Young

This is the only restaurant built on the Arkansas River between Colorado and Mississippi. The main entrance is an old lighthouse tower. Seafood is the specialty at this unique dining spot which is open for dinner every day, except Sunday. Take Fort Smith Exit from I-40 and go to 6201 Midland Boulevard (U.S. Highways 64 and 71). Hugh Ballard is the owner-manager.

Nutty Puppies

2 ounces chopped	3 cups corn meal
Spanish peanuts	1½ cups flour
1 No. 303 can of cream	1¾ teaspoons salt
style corn	½ teaspoon black
2 ounces crumbled	pepper
bacon	1⅓ cups buttermilk
1 or 2 jalapeño peppers,	½ cup water
chopped fine	⅓ pound melted butter
1 medium onion,	3 eggs
chopped	Deep fat for frying

Combine ingredients well, roll into 36 one-ounce rolls. Fry in 450° deep fat until golden brown. Serve piping hot with seafood dishes.

ANDERSON'S CAJUN'S WHARF
Little Rock, Arkansas • illustration by Randall McKissick

Four years ago, Bruce Anderson converted a warehouse on the Arkansas River into a beautiful restaurant that captures the Cajun atmosphere of old New Orleans. Dinner served from 5 to 10:30 p.m. weekdays, until 11 p.m. Saturday. Not open Sunday, Thanksgiving and Christmas Days. Located at 2400 Cantrell. Take the Markham exit off Interstate 30 to Cantrell Road, turn right and go three miles.

Oysters Bienville

In 3 tablespoons butter, sauté the following diced ingredients: 8 green onions, 1 cup raw mushrooms and 1½ cups shrimp. Add ¾ cup Chablis and simmer for 20 minutes over medium heat. Add 1½ cups chicken consommé and cook for 10 minutes more. Blend 3 tablespoons flour in a little water and then add to sauce, stirring until it thickens. Beat 2 egg yolks with 2 tablespoons cream, then add 2 tablespoons oyster juice. Add this mixture slowly to sauce and cook over low heat for 15 minutes, stirring constantly. Season to taste with white pepper and Tabasco. Cover 36 raw oysters in the shell with sauce and bake for 7 minutes in 350° oven. Top each with sprinkle of Parmesan, dot of butter and bake 1 minute. Serves 6.

RESTAURANT JACQUES & SUZANNE
Little Rock, Arkansas • illustration by Ted Lewin

The authentic French-Swiss cuisine is prepared by six chefs trained in Europe. The restaurant is downtown on the 30th floor of the First National Building at Capitol and Broadway Avenues and affords diners a spectacular view of the city. Lunch is served Monday through Friday and dinner every day, except Sunday. Reservations advisable.

Vinaigrette Salad Sauce

½ small onion, chopped
⅝ cup tarragon vinegar, plus a few of the tarragon leaves
1 tablespoon Dijon French mustard
½ teaspoon Worcestershire sauce
Dash of Tabasco
1 large clove of garlic
Freshly ground pepper
1 whole egg
⅔ cup olive oil
1 beef bouillon cube
3 tablespoons boiling water
1⅓ cups vegetable oil (corn or safflower)
Salt to taste

Place chopped onion, vinegar, tarragon leaves, mustard, Worcestershire sauce, Tabasco, garlic, pepper and egg in blender and blend well. Slowly add the olive oil. Add the beef bouillon cube after it has dissolved in the water and blend quickly. Blend in the salad oil, adding it in a gradual stream. Taste before adding salt. Place dressing in covered jar and refrigerate, although the dressing will be more flavorful if not icy cold when served. Dress salad greens at the last minute. Makes 3 cups of dressing.

HAYS HOUSE
Council Grove, Kansas • illustration by Joan Solmes

This restaurant has been in operation since 1857. Its present owners, Helen and Charles Judd, boast that it is the oldest continuously operating restaurant west of the Mississippi. The original building has been restored, revealing skilled construction using native walnut, oak and stone. It is noted for its home cooking and excellent baked goods. Open every day from 6 a.m. to 9 p.m.; reservations requested. Closed Christmas and New Year's days. The restaurant is at 112 West Main Street.

Crunchy Chicken Salad

5 cups cold chicken (or
   turkey) chunks
1 cup celery, stalks cut in
   ¼-inch slices
½ cup sliced water
   chestnuts
1 cup pineapple tidbits
⅔ cup mayonnaise

⅔ cup sour cream
⅓ cup pineapple juice
½ teaspoon Lawry's
   Seasoned Salt
1 tablespoon sugar
6 cantaloupe or
   pineapple rings, or
   tomato wedges

Mix the chicken or turkey with celery, water chestnuts
and pineapple. Combine mayonnaise, sour cream,
pineapple juice, salt and sugar. Toss salad with
dressing and serve in cantaloupe or pineapple rings
or with tomato wedges. Serves 6.

Cranberry-Strawberry Pie

1 pound fresh
   cranberries, frozen
2 cups sugar
2 cups frozen
   strawberries, sliced
8 tablespoons cherry
   gelatin
¾ cup finely diced celery
1 cup black walnut
   pieces

½ pound large
   marshmallows
½ cup milk
3 cups prepared
   whipped topping
2 graham cracker pie
   shells, baked and
   frozen

Grind frozen cranberries, mix with sugar and let stand
several hours. Drain juice, mix with juice from
thawed strawberries to make 2 cups. Heat juices, then
stir in gelatin until dissolved. Cool until slightly
thickened, then fold in cranberries, strawberries,
celery and walnuts. Cut marshmallows into small
pieces and melt over hot water with milk. Cool, then
fold into gelatin mixture with whipped topping. Pour
into pie shells and chill until serving time. (Frozen pie
shells make for easier cutting.)

COWTOWN CLUB
Dodge City, Kansas • illustration by Don Odle

As the name implies, this Western restaurant
thrives in a town made famous by cattlemen and such
colorful characters as Bat Masterson and Billy the Kid.
Visitors to the city are still impressed by the area's
huge numbers of cattle being fattened for market and
for the great beef served at the Cowtown Club by
owners Grant and Susie Parsons. Dinner served
every day, except Sunday and Monday. Reservations
necessary. It is one block south and six blocks west of
famous Boot Hill at 503 East Trail.

Marinated Beef Loin

Many cattlemen like their beef to be marinated
before being charcoal broiled. This is the way it is
done at the club.

Marinate a tenderloin of beef for four hours or longer
in the following mixture:

1 10-ounce bottle
   Worcestershire sauce
1 10-ounce bottle soy
   sauce

20 ounces water
1 medium onion, sliced

Place in bowl and make sure meat is covered by
marinade, or turned frequently if it does not cover.
Place in refrigerator. Remove meat from mixture and
broil on charcoal grill until done to taste. Slice and
serve.

JUDGE RIGGS RESTAURANT
Wichita, Kansas • illustration by Max Altekruse

Located in the Wichita Hilton Hotel, this interesting
restaurant is named for Wichita's first judge, Reuben
Riggs. It is famous for its fine food and singing waiters
and waitresses, most of whom are local college

students. Open for lunch and dinner every day. Overnight accommodations and recreation facilities available in the hotel; reservations advisable. From the Kansas Turnpike, take the East Wichita Exit and drive 10 blocks west on U.S. 54. The restaurant is at the corner of East Kellogg and Rock Road.

Pretzel Pie

Combine 1½ cups salted pretzel crumbs with ¾ cup of sugar and ¾ cup of melted butter. Press into two 9-inch pie pans. For the filling use soft butter-brickle ice cream. Freeze pie and make meringue. Combine 1 cup water, 2 cups sugar and 2 teaspoons cream of tartar. Bring to a rolling boil for 3 minutes. Remove from fire. Whip 8 room-temperature egg whites to a wet peak, adding 1 tablespoon of sugar slowly. When egg whites are at a dry peak, add sugar and water liquid slowly. Take pie out of freezer, spread on meringue *quickly* and put under broiler to brown. (Oven must be hot!) Return pies to freezer until frozen. At serving time, cut and serve immediately.

MASHBURN RESTAURANT
Hammond, Louisiana • illustration by Linda Boston

Surrounded by 18 acres of landscaped gardens, this fine dining spot, which features New Orleans cuisine, is in a farmhouse built in 1907. On U.S. 190 East, it is three miles from Hammond, and is an hour's drive from New Orleans. Dinner served every day, except Monday, Christmas and New Year's Day and July 4. Lunch on Sunday only. Reservations advisable. The Jack Mashburn family owns and operates this delightful place.

Trout with Crayfish Sauce

Poach six 8-ounce filets of trout in 2 quarts of water, 1 teaspoon lemon juice, 1 tablespoon white wine

and 2 tablespoons Season-all, 2 bay leaves and a pinch of tarragon. Place poached trout on plates and pour crayfish sauce (below) on each portion. Serves 6.

Crayfish Sauce

1 pound cooked crayfish   *1 tablespoon flour*
   tails (or lobster tails),   *2 cups half and half*
   bite-size pieces   *2 tablespoons cream*
¼ pound butter   *sherry*
2 tablespoons chopped
   parsley

Sauté parsley in melted butter, till soft, then add flour, stirring until lumps are out. Add half and half, stir over heat until thick, then add sherry and crayfish pieces.

Broccoli Hollandaise

Boil 24 spears of broccoli until tender in slightly salted water, with lemon juice, butter and pepper. In a double boiler mix 6 egg yolks, 6 teaspoons lemon juice and ¼ pound butter, stir with wooden spoon until thick or to desired thickness. Place 4 spears of broccoli on each plate and pour sauce over them. Serves 6.

LA PROVENCE
Lacombe, Louisiana • illustration by Fred W. Thomas

Constantin Kerageorgiou, who was born in Provence, France, is the chef and proprietor of this delightful French country restaurant 40 miles north of New Orleans. It is on U.S. Highway 190, between Mandeville and Lacombe, about 10 miles from Interstate 12. Dinner is served Wednesday through Monday from 5 to 11 p.m. Sunday serving hours are 1 to 9 p.m. Closed Tuesday. Reservations necessary.

Poulet Fromage

3½ pound chicken, cut into pieces	Salt and pepper, to taste
3 tablespoons butter	2 tablespoons grated Swiss cheese
2 teaspoons chopped shallots	1 tablespoon crumbled blue cheese
½ cup dry vermouth	1 tablespoon Dijon mustard
¾ cup whipping cream	

Sauté chicken in 2 tablespoons butter, *but do not brown.* Add chopped shallots and dry vermouth. Cook until liquid reduces slightly, add enough whipping cream to almost cover chicken. Season with salt and pepper. Bring to a boil. Put in oven and cover with aluminum foil. Bake in 475° oven for about 15 minutes. Remove chicken pieces, strain sauce and cook until it reduces. Whip in cheeses, additional tablespoon of butter and mustard. When sauce is smooth, pour over chicken and serve with rice pilaf. Serves 4.

Baked Oysters John Batiste Reboul

1 pint freshly shucked oysters	2 ounces shallots or white part of green onion, chopped fine
1½ pounds fresh mushrooms, chopped	½ cup dry white wine
2 tablespoons butter	2 bay leaves
4 cloves garlic, chopped fine	Pinch of thyme
	Salt and pepper, to taste
	1 cup hollandaise sauce

Sauté chopped mushrooms in butter; add chopped garlic and shallots. Add wine, bay leaves and seasonings. Cook sauce until reduced. Place fresh oysters in a buttered casserole and top with mushroom sauce and bake in 450° oven, about 7-8 minutes, until oysters are done. Cover with hollandaise sauce and brown under broiler. Serves 6.

THE BON TON
New Orleans, Louisiana • illustration by Larry McManus

Alvin Pierce, the owner of this charming bistro, is a Cajun from the banks of Bayou Lafourche, about 60 miles from New Orleans. All of the recipes used in the restaurant are old family recipes. Open for lunch and dinner Monday through Friday. Reservations necessary for dinner. Closed weekends. It is at 401 Magazine Street in downtown New Orleans.

Alzina's Bread Pudding

1 loaf stale French bread	2 tablespoons vanilla
1 quart milk	1 cup raisins
3 eggs	3 tablespoons butter, melted
2 cups sugar	

Soak bread in milk; crush with hands until well-mixed. Add eggs, sugar, vanilla, raisins. Stir well. Pour melted butter in bottom of heavy pan; pour in bread mixture. Bake in 350° oven for about 40 minutes or until firm. Let cool; then cut into squares. Place in individual oven-proof dessert dishes. When ready to serve add Whiskey Sauce (below); heat under broiler.

Whiskey Sauce

Cream 1 stick of butter with 1 cup of sugar. Cook mixture in a double boiler until it is very hot and well dissolved. Then add 1 beaten egg and whip very fast so that egg doesn't curdle. Let cool and add 2 to 3 ouces of bourbon, to taste.

Dirty Rice

Grind ½ dozen chicken livers, ½ dozen chicken gizzards, 1 large onion, 1 green pepper and 2 stalks of celery. In a cast iron skillet put 2 tablespoons olive oil, let heat. Add ground ingredients and 1 teaspoon salt and 1 teaspoon black pepper. Cook about 1 hour in an uncovered pan, or until all drippings are absorbed. Add ¼ cup chopped parsley and about 3 cups cooked rice, mix well and cook about 10 more minutes. Serves 8.

CHRISTIAN'S RESTAURANT

New Orleans, Louisiana • illustration by Mary Beth Schwark

Christian Ansel, the owner, spent eight years working in his family's famous restaurant — Galatoire's — on Bourbon Street before deciding to open a small place of his own in a quaint old church in the mid-city area. A fine chef, Roland Huet, presides over the kitchen, turning out great traditional French dishes. Lunch served Monday through Friday 11:30 a.m. to 2 p.m. and dinner 5:30 to 10 p.m. every day except Sunday. Reservations necessary. The address is 3835 Iberville Street.

Redfish Froid with Horseradish Sauce

*6 3-ounce filets of
    redfish or other
    boneless fish*

Poach the fish, and cool in court bouillon (below) overnight in refrigerator. Drain fish and serve on a bed of finely chopped lettuce, topped with horseradish sauce (below). Serves 6 as an appetizer.

Court Bouillon

Combine following ingredients in a deep saucepan: 1 stalk celery (sliced), 3 sprigs parsley, 1 bay leaf, 2 coarsely chopped carrots, 1 sliced lemon, 1 teaspoon salt, 2 quarts water, 10 bruised peppercorns, 1 pinch thyme, 1 large white onion (sliced), 1 cup dry white wine and ¼ cup cider vinegar. Simmer uncovered for 20 minutes. Strain liquid through a fine sieve.

Horseradish Sauce

Combine 2 cups commercial sour cream, blended well with 1½ cups thoroughly drained horseradish, ⅓ cup chopped pecans, salt and pepper, to taste. Chill until served.

LOG HOUSE

Biloxi, Mississippi • illustration by Richard Young

Mary and Jim Myers provide fine regional food at reasonable prices. Open every day from 6 a.m. to 10 p.m. Closed Thanksgiving and Christmas. The restaurant is midway between Gulfport and Biloxi at 190 DeBuys Road (U.S. Highway 90).

Log House Gumbo

*1½ cups chopped
    onions
1 cup chopped celery
½ cup chopped green
    pepper
6 tablespoons oil
1½ tablespoons flour
1 quart water
2 bay leaves
1 tablespoon ketchup
1 tablespoon minced
    garlic*

*Pinch of red pepper
Pinch of black pepper
1 tablespoon
    Worcestershire sauce
¼ teaspoon Tabasco
    sauce
Salt to taste
1 No. 2 can okra
2 cups canned tomatoes
1 pound cleaned raw
    shrimp
½ pound fresh crab meat
1½ teaspoons gumbo
    filé*

Braise onions, celery and green pepper in 2 tablespoons of oil. In a separate pot mix 4 tablespoons of oil with flour. Brown well to make a French roux. Add water, bay leaves, ketchup, garlic, red and black pepper, Worchestershire sauce and Tabasco sauce to vegetable mixture. Salt to taste. Cook gently until vegetables are done and flavors well blended. Then add okra, tomatoes, shrimp and crab. Thicken with roux and simmer briefly, adding water as needed, until the seafood is done. Add gumbo filé and serve over rice. Makes 6 portions.

THE WHITE PILLARS
Biloxi, Mississippi • illustration by Karen Bayer

Reminiscent of the antebellum South, this house, of masonry and handmade brick, was built around the turn of the century and patterned after the famous Gunston Hall in Virginia. There are seven antique-filled dining rooms and a lounge. Dinner is served by reservation only. Closed on Thanksgiving and Christmas Day. The address is 100 Rodenburg Avenue in Biloxi. Virginia Mladinich is the owner-manager.

Crab Mushrooms

1 pound lump crab meat	½ cup grated sharp
4 tablespoons butter	Cheddar
4 tablespoons flour	Pinch nutmeg, salt and
1½ cups heavy cream	white pepper
1 cup light cream	¼ cup dry white wine
2 tablespoons grated	8 giant mushrooms
Parmesan cheese	

In the top of a double boiler, melt butter and blend in flour, stirring constantly. Slowly add cream, grated cheeses, seasonings, wine and crab meat. Sauté mushrooms in a little butter, garlic and wine. Place sautéed mushrooms in a baking dish and pour cream mixture over mushrooms. Sprinkle additional grated cheese over the top and place in 400° oven until the mixture bubbles. If desired, garnish top with sautéed mushroom halves.

AL BAKER'S
Clayton, Missouri • illustration by Frederick Carter

Continental cuisine served with Midwestern friendliness is the winning combination of this restaurant at 8101 Clayton Road in Clayton, a western suburb of St. Louis. Take U.S. 40 west out of St. Louis to the Brentwood North exit. The wine cellar, dating back to 1919, contains over 125,000 bottles from fine European and California vineyards. Dinner served every weekday. Closed Sunday and holidays, and the first two weeks of July.

Rigatoni with Broccoli

In a large saucepan bring to a boil 2 quarts of water which has been liberally salted. Add an 8- to 12-ounce package of rigatoni pasta. Cook 9-11 minutes until it is soft. In another saucepan, bring 1 cup salted water to a boil then add 6 stalks of fresh broccoli. Cook until soft. Remove from water, drain and cut flowers from stalks. With the back of a fork mash flowers slightly to form a paste. In a sauté pan put two pats of butter and 6 ounces of fresh sliced mushrooms. Sauté lightly. Drain cooked pasta, leaving very little water in the pan. Add ¼ pound of sweet, softened butter, fresh ground pepper, sautéed mushrooms and mashed broccoli flowers to the pasta. Sprinkle mixture liberally with 1 cup imported, freshly ground Parmesan cheese. Toss together until completely mixed. Serves 3-4.

LODGE OF THE FOUR SEASONS
Lake Ozark, Missouri • illustration by Joan Solmes

More than 200 acres make up this year-round resort on Lake Ozark in southern Missouri. There are complete vacation facilities — golf, tennis, boating, horseback riding and a complete health spa. Dining

rooms are open for breakfast, lunch and dinner every day. Reservations necessary. Take U.S. Highway 54 south from I-70 to Lake Ozark.

Carrot Cake

2 cups sugar	*1 teaspoon salt*
1½ cups cooking oil	*2 teaspoons cinnamon*
4 eggs	*3 cups grated carrots*
2 cups cake flour	*1 cup chopped pecans*
2 teaspoons soda	

Put sugar, oil and eggs in a mixing bowl and beat well. Sift the flour, soda, salt and cinnamon together and add to mixture slowly while beating. After it is well blended, add carrots and pecans. Pour batter into 3 greased, 9-inch layer cake pans. Preheat oven to 325° and bake for 30-45 minutes. Cool on racks, then ice with frosting (below).

Frosting

Mix ½ pound soft butter with 8 ounces of cream cheese; when well blended, slowly blend in 1 pound of confectioners' sugar and 2 teaspoons vanilla.

OLD MISSOURI HOMESTEAD
Sedalia, Missouri • illustration by Doug Jackson

This restaurant is a re-created country home in the heart of Sedalia, at Fifth Street and Lamine Avenue. The owner, Mrs. Okee Rice, built the restaurant in 1943 to bring country cooking to town when gas rationing curtailed driving. Dinner served 5 to 11:30 p.m. every day, except Sunday. Closed most holidays. Reservations advisable.

Ham Virginia

Melt ¼ cup butter in a heavy skillet. Sauté a thick slice of cooked smoked ham in the butter until the ham is browned on both sides. Transfer ham to a heated platter and keep warm. To the skillet add 4 tablespoons brown sugar and 1 cup of sherry. Stir over a low flame until the sugar melts. Add 2 tablespoons flour which has been mixed into a paste with 4 tablespoons of water. Cook, stirring constantly, until the sauce is thick and smooth. Return ham to the skillet and simmer in sauce for about 10 minutes, turning ham to cook on both sides. Arrange ham on warm platter and top with remaining sauce.

NOAH'S ARK
St. Charles, Missouri • illustration by Joan Solmes

This unusual restaurant is a representation of the famed ark and carries out the theme with stuffed animal displays in the dining areas. It is open for breakfast, lunch and dinner every day; overnight accommodations and recreation facilities. Reservations advisable for hotel rooms. Take the Fairlane Exit from I-70 and proceed to 1500 South Fifth Street in downtown St. Charles. James G. Kennedy is the manager; Paul Edgar McDowell is the executive chef.

Noah's Ark Bread Pudding with Vanilla Sauce

4 cups toasted bread crumbs	¼ cup coconut
4 cups warm milk	¼ cup raisins
1 cup sugar	4 ounces soft butter or margarine
¼ teaspoon nutmeg	1 teaspoon vanilla
¼ teaspoon salt	9 eggs

Combine all of the above ingredients except eggs, and mix ingredients well. Beat eggs separately until light and beat into mixture. Pour into a 4-quart buttered casserole and place in a pan of warm water in a 350° oven for about 1 hour, or until golden brown and pudding is set. Serve warm with Vanilla Sauce (below).

Vanilla Sauce

Whip together until light and fluffy, 9 ounces soft vanilla ice cream, 9 ounces Cool Whip and ½ teaspoon vanilla. Serves 8-10.

Poached Pacific Northwest Salmon with Green Peppercorn Sauce

6 7-ounce filets of red salmon	1 bay leaf
1 quart water	2 tablespoons each: chopped onion, celery
1 teaspoon lemon juice	and carrot
1 tablespoon white wine	Pinch of dill and salt

Mix water, lemon juice, wine, vegetables and seasonings. Place salmon in mixture — it should be just covered — and place on burner on top of stove. Bring just to a boil and remove from fire. Makes 6 portions. Serve with Green Peppercorn Sauce (below).

Green Peppercorn Sauce

Whip together 1½ cups hot medium cream sauce, ¼ cup dry white wine, few drops of Tabasco, salt and pepper, to taste, 1½ tablespoons hard butter and 2 tablespoons green peppercorns (can be found in gourmet food departments). After ingredients are well whipped together serve over the poached salmon that has been placed on a heated platter. Serves 6.

AL'S RESTAURANT
St. Louis, Missouri • illustration by Skip Starr

This fine waterfront restaurant is famous with local gourmets for its excellent food. Dinner is the only meal. Closed Sunday and major holidays and the first two weeks in July. Reservations advisable. Take any exit to Jefferson National Memorial (Riverfront), proceed north to Biddle Street, then go west one block to 1200 North Main Street. Albert Barroni is the owner and manager.

Rissoto alla Milanese

Bring 6 cups of chicken stock to a boil. Sauté 1 medium chopped onion in 4 tablespoons butter until tender. Add 1 cup chopped mushrooms and cook at a very low temperature, stirring frequently. Add 1 cup raw rice and cook, stirring until the grains glisten with the butter and are somewhat opaque. Pour in ½ cup dry white wine and cook until it is completely absorbed. Stir in ¼ teaspoon saffron. Lower heat under the chicken stock to simmering and gradually add to rice mixture a cup at a time, stirring rice after each addition until almost all liquid is absorbed. Continue until rice is tender and nearly all stock has been used. Stir in ¼ cup Parmesan cheese. Serves 6.

Toasted Ravioli

A unique St. Louis favorite, this dish starts with the traditional small meat pies in pasta dough. The frozen bite-size ravioli squares are dipped into a batter of ½ cup of milk and 2 eggs beaten, and dredged in bread crumbs and then deep-fried in 350° fat for 3-4 minutes or until they are brown and rise to the top. Immediately after they come out of the fryer they are sprinkled liberally with grated Parmesan cheese and served as appetizers. For a main course version, the crisp, toasted ravioli are topped with Italian tomato or meat sauce.

Zabaione

5 egg yolks, plus	*2 tablespoons sugar*
1 whole egg	*½ cup marsala wine*

Combine egg yolks, whole egg and sugar in the top of a double boiler above simmering water. Beat the mixture with a wire whisk or a rotary beater until it is pale yellow and fluffy. Then gradually pour in the marsala and continue beating until the zabaione becomes thick enough to hold its shape in a spoon. This process may take as long as 10 minutes. Spoon mixture into dessert bowls or long-stemmed glasses and serve while it is still hot. Makes 4 portions.

CHASE PARK PLAZA HOTEL
St. Louis, Missouri • illustration by James T. Stelma

The Koplar family owns and operates this fine old hotel at 212 N. Kings Highway, midway between St. Louis and Washington Universities. There are four dining rooms and two night clubs in the hotel. Breakfast, lunch and dinner served in most of the dining rooms daily. Reservations advisable.

Pepperloin Steak

Rub a 4-pound beef tenderloin on both sides with freshly ground black pepper and rock salt. Place meat in pan with 1 bay leaf, 2 onions, sliced, and 1 crushed clove of garlic. Cover with ½ cup of oil. Marinate in refrigerator for 2-3 days, turn once or twice. Drain and sear over charcoal fire. Finish over slow heat for about 25 minutes. Slice and serve with Mustard Sauce (below). Serves 8-10.

Mustard Sauce

Sauté 3 tablespoons chopped onions and 2 chopped shallots or green onions in a tablespoon of butter. Add ½ crushed garlic clove, 2 ounces white wine, 12 parsley sprigs, 1 bay leaf, 1 clove, 1 tablespoon brown sugar, 1 cup cider vinegar, 3 tablespoons dry mustard and ½ cup prepared mustard. Mix ingredients well, then add a pinch of thyme and oregano and 4 cups of demi-glaze or brown gravy. Cook slowly for 30 minutes, then strain, and add a dash of Tabasco.

Stuffed Tomatoes

4 medium tomatoes	*Chopped parsley, salt,*
2 ounces butter	*pepper, nutmeg and*
1 ounce diced shallots	*MSG, to taste*
8 ounces sliced, fresh	*1 teaspoon flour*
mushrooms	*2 ounces chicken stock*
1 ounce dry white wine	*1 ounce heavy cream*
	1 cup hollandaise sauce
	(optional)
	Parmesan cheese

Scoop out insides of tomatoes. Heat butter in a skillet, add shallots and sauté until they are halfway done. Add sliced mushrooms; braise for about 3 minutes and add wine, chopped parsley and seasonings and cook until all fluid is gone. Dust flour over mixture and stir well. Add chicken stock and cook for 4 minutes over low heat. Stir in cream and stuff tomatoes. Bake in 350° oven for 15 minutes, then sprinkle with grated Parmesan cheese and broil until browned. May be topped with hollandaise sauce, if desired. Makes 4 portions.

SCHNEITHORST'S HOFAMBERG INN
St. Louis, Missouri • illustration by Steve Takenaga

This charming old Bavarian-type restaurant, filled with antiques, is owned and managed by the Arthur Schneithorst family, which has been in the restaurant business for three generations. Across the street from the Frontenac Plaza Shopping Center, the inn is one block south of U.S. 40 at 1600 Lindbergh Boulevard. Lunch and dinner served every day, except Christmas.

Veal à la Strausburg

2 pounds veal steak
2 eggs, slightly beaten
2 tablespoons milk
2 cups crushed corn
 flakes

1 cup canned sliced
 mushrooms and juice
1 tablespoon flour,
 mixed with water
2 to 3 ounces sherry
Salt, pepper to taste

Have veal steak cut ½ or ¾ inch thick. Cut into pieces. Dip veal into mixture of egg and milk. Roll in cereal. Brown in hot fat, then add mushrooms and liquid. Cover and cook very slowly until tender, about 50 minutes. Thicken gravy with flour mixed with water. Add Sherry and seasonings. Serve with Veal Steaks. Serves 5-6.

PHOENICIA CLUB AND RESTAURANT
Tulsa, Oklahoma • illustration by Harvey Kidder

Since its opening in 1964 this Middle Eastern transplant with its Lebanese foods and decor has been an oasis for seekers of interesting cuisine. Good food in a relaxing atmosphere is the aim of owner Don Abraham. Open daily for lunch and dinner except Sundays. Address is 3525-H East 51st Street off I-44.

Phoenicia Beef Kabob

1 pound beef tenderloin
16 mushroom caps
2 onions, cut in eighths
2 tomatoes, cut in
 eighths

1 green pepper, cut in
 pieces
Melted butter
½ lemon
Worcestershire sauce

Cut beef in 2-inch cubes. Thread on four skewers. Place vegetables in flat pan, sprinkle with salt and pepper and arrange skewers on top. Dribble with melted butter and broil 5 minutes. Turn skewers and broil to desired doneness. Remove meat from skewers, mix with vegetables and squeeze on lemon juice and few dashes Worcestershire. Return to broiler 3 minutes. Serve over hot rice. Serves 4.

Hommos Tahini

Drain 1-pound can garbanzo beans. Run through food mill. Mix with small garlic clove mashed with ½ teaspoon salt, 3 tablespoons Tahini (ground sesame seeds) and juice of 2 lemons. Mix well. Cover surface with 1 tablespoon olive oil, garnish with paprika and snipped parsley. Serve as appetizer dip with crackers and vegetables.

CONFEDERATE HOUSE
Houston, Texas • illustration by Bob Rozas

The focal point of this dining room is a portrait of Robert E. Lee flanked by a collection of historic Confederate flags. There are also displays of buttons, sabers and other Civil War memorabilia. It is open for lunch and dinner every day. The address is 4007 Westheimer, and it is one mile east of the Galleria Shopping Mall. Take the 610 Loop from the Southwest Freeway. Gordon Edge is the owner-manager. Reservations advisable.

Confederate Pie

5 egg yolks
1¾ cups sugar
2 tablespoons corn meal
1 tablespoon flour

½ cup melted butter
1 cup milk
2 teaspoons lemon juice
9-inch unbaked pie shell

Beat egg yolks with 1 cup of the sugar. In another bowl mix remaining ¾ cup of sugar with corn meal, flour and melted butter. Mix well, then add milk. Combine two mixtures. Add lemon juice, stir well. Pour into unbaked pie shell and bake in 350° oven until filling is set, about 45 minutes. Serve hot.

PADRE ISLAND BEACH HOTEL
Padre Island, Texas • illustration by Robert E. Lee

In the area of the Padre Island National Seashore and the King Ranch, this hotel on the Gulf of Mexico has complete vacation facilities and an excellent dining room, The Veranda. Breakfast, lunch and dinner served daily; overnight accommodations. Fishing trips daily. Reservations advisable. From Corpus Christi, go south on Padre Island Drive to the island. Then turn left on Windward Drive to the Gulf.

Chef Brikowski's Seafood Salad

2 pounds Alaska crabmeat	1 cup mayonnaise
1 8-ounce can chunk pineapple	½ lemon, juice
1 4-ounce can sliced, cooked mushrooms	2 tablespoons horseradish
	3 tablespoons sugar

Cube crabmeat, add drained pineapple and mushrooms. Add remaining ingredients. Serve with starred tomato and boiled egg slices. Serves 6.

Padre Island Stuffed Shrimp

¼ cup bell pepper, chopped	1 teaspoon seafood seasoning
½ cup minced onion	½ cup chopped crab meat
½ cup diced celery	
¼ cup butter or margarine	1 pound shrimp, size 16/20
1 cup chicken broth	Cornbread (below)
1 teaspoon sage	Cooking oil

Sauté pepper, onion and celery in melted butter in large skillet 5 minutes. Add chicken broth and set aside. Crumble cornbread into large bowl. Add skillet ingredients, sage, seafood seasoning and crab meat and mix well. Clean and "butterfly" cut the shrimp. Cover each shrimp individually with mixture, surrounding completely. Deep fry in cooking oil at 350° until golden brown.

Southern Corn Bread

Sift together 1½ cups flour, ¾ cup yellow cornmeal, 2 tablespoons sugar, 4½ teaspoons baking powder and 1 teaspoon salt into large bowl. Add 1 beaten egg, ⅔ cup milk and ⅓ cup melted butter or oil. Turn into 8-inch square pan. Bake at 400° for 30 to 40 minutes or until done. Cool and crumble for stuffing mixture.

JOE COTTEN'S BARBECUE
Robstown, Texas • illustration by Robert Boston

For over 30 years barbecue lovers have been flocking to this spot for beef, spareribs, pork and sausages cooked in pits over a mesquite wood fire. The four dining rooms are decorated with antiques and there are porch swings and rockers for guests to relax in. The helicopter landing pad is a touch of the 20th century. Owner Joe Cotten, a friendly, homespun host, is a legend in south Texas. Nearby tourist attractions are Corpus Christi and Padre Island. It is on U.S. Highway 77 (South) in Robstown.

Cotten's Original Barbecue Sauce

23 ounces tomato juice	¼ jalapeño pepper, diced
⅔ cup ketchup	
2 tablespoons mustard	½ teaspoon salt
2 tablespoons Worcestershire sauce	½ teaspoon pepper
	1 tablespoon margarine
2 tablespoons finely diced onion	2 tablespoons lemon juice

Put all ingredients in a pan and cook at slow boil with lid on for about 30 minutes. Use as a sauce for cooked meat.

FIG TREE RESTAURANT
San Antonio, Texas • illustration by Warren Hunter

A century-old home has been converted into a restaurant along the famed Paseo del Rio in downtown San Antonio. Dinner is served every day both indoors and on the outdoor riverside terrace. Reservations necessary. Closed Thanksgiving and Christmas. Frank Phelps is the owner.

English Mix

Melt 2 tablespoons butter in a hot skillet. Add 2 slices of green pepper, a slice of sweet onion and ½ teaspoon fresh cilantro. Sauté lightly. To this add the following: 2 ounces beef tenderloin, 2 ounces loin of lamb, 2 ounces boned chicken breast, 1 ounce chicken liver and 1 ounce of country sausage. Over these ingredients pour ½ ounce of Cointreau and a large fresh mushroom, thinly sliced. Sauté to desired degree of doneness. Serves 1.

Oyster Beef

Slice 7 ounces beef tenderloin about ¼-inch thick. Place in skillet with ¼ jigger brandy along with 1 ounce of fresh oyster liquor. Sauté to desired degree. At the last few seconds, add 1 fresh oyster and cook lightly. Remove from skillet and top the steak with the oyster. Makes 1 portion.

MOSSCLIFF
San Marcos, Texas • illustration by Allen Rich

This unusual restaurant is located in the country on the Post Road, a mile north of the city of San Marcos. There is a garden dining room, a "pillow room" where diners sit at low tables on giant pillows, and a regular dining room. Guests are invited to stroll through the formal gardens. Open 11 a.m. to 10:30 p.m. Monday through Friday; 3 p.m. to 10:30 p.m. on weekends. Walt Schmeltekopf is the genial host.

Blueberry Muffins

1½ cups flour	*1 egg*
½ cup sugar	*½ cup milk*
2 teaspoons baking powder	*¼ cup shortening, melted*
½ teaspoon salt	*1 cup fresh blueberries*

Sift dry ingredients, then moisten with the combined egg, milk and shortening. Stir enough to thoroughly blend then fold in blueberries. Bake in well greased muffin pans in a 400° oven 20-25 minutes. Makes 12 large muffins.

Holiday Duck Mosscliff

Drain a 17-ounce can of Bing cherries. Pour 1 cup tawny port wine over cherries and let stand overnight. Wash and quarter two 4-pound ducks. Broil skin side up until all fat is off — about 20 minutes. Roast in 350° oven for 30 minutes. Combine ¼ cup fresh orange juice with 2 tablespoons cornstarch — make a smooth paste, then stir into port-soaked cherries. Cook mixture until sauce is thick and clear, then add 4 tablespoons sugar. Brush sauce over duckling. Serve with hot cherry sauce. Makes 6 portions.

Poppyseed Dressing

1 ½ cups sugar
2 teaspoons dry mustard
2 teaspoons salt
⅔ cup vinegar (not wine)

3 tablespoons onion juice
2 cups Wesson oil
3 tablespoons poppyseeds

Mix sugar, mustard, salt and vinegar together. Add onion juice and stir thoroughly. While beating add oil *slowly* and continue beating until thick. Then add poppyseeds. Chill and serve over fresh fruit salad. Makes about 1 quart of dressing.

THE GLASS MENAGERIE
Woodlands, Texas • illustration by Nell Boyle

The menu is mostly French and Texan with a pinch of New Orleans. Chef Keith Saunders came here by way of Europe and a Creole restaurant in America. The greenhouse-like restaurant is on the wharf at Woodlands, a new town 25 miles northwest of Houston. Lunch and dinner served every day, except Sunday and Monday.

Lobster Thermidor

2 lobsters, 1½ pounds each
2 finely chopped shallots, or green onions

1 tablespoon butter
4-6 ounces dry white wine
8 ounces half and half
2 cups white sauce

1 teaspoon salt
Pinch each of cayenne, white pepper and chervil
1 teaspoon dry mustard

½ cup grated Gruyère cheese
Halved stuffed olives, lemon slices and parsley, for garnish

Boil lobsters in water for 18 minutes. Cut in half and break off claws. Remove meat from shells and set half shells aside for stuffing. Cut lobster into 1-inch pieces. Brown shallots or onions in butter, then add white wine and let boil until reduced. Slowly stir in half and half, and white sauce. Add salt, cayenne, white pepper and chervil. Simmer until mixture coats a spoon, add lobster and cook for 2 minutes. Remove from fire and add moistened mustard and ¾ of the cheese. Fill shells with mixture and sprinkle with remaining cheese. Glaze in hot oven or under broiler for 1 minute until golden brown. Garnish and serve 4.

West

Elegant Chocolate Cheese Cake – Steinbeck House, California
Green Papaya Soup – Coconut Palace, Hawaii
Cappucino – Hole In The Wall, Nevada
Cioppino – North Beach Restaurant, California

KAY'S KITCHEN

Ketchikan, Alaska • Illustration by Lin Ervine

Kay and Eric Gundersen turned a waterfront home into a flourishing restaurant and gift shop. In addition to the indoor dining room, there are tables on the outdoor deck which provide diners with a magnificent view of the boat harbor and neighboring channel islands. Lunch is served daily 11 a.m. to 4 p.m.; reservations advisable. Closed Sunday and Monday and from April 1 to the third Tuesday in June. It is located at 2813 Tongass on State Highway 7 on the west side of town.

French Steakette

Take 6 serving-size pieces of tenderized round steak, sprinkle with salt and pepper. Dip each piece of meat in 1 cup of flour mixed with 1 tablespoon garlic powder. Brown meat pieces in a frying pan in ½ cup cooking oil. When meat is browned remove to an open baking pan. Pour 1 cup white wine, 1 cup water, ¼ cup dehydrated onions and 1 tablespoon chopped parsley into frying pan used for browning. Simmer mixture until thickened, then pour over steakettes in baking pan. Bake uncovered in 350° oven for 1 hour or until meat is tender.

ETIENNE'S FRENCH RESTAURANT

Paradise Valley, Arizona • illustration by Don McGovern

Superb French food is served in a charming dining room; entrées are prepared to order. Dinner is served every day except Sunday. Lunch is also served Tuesday through Saturday. Reservations necessary. The Gluck family are the owners and managers. It is in the La Posada Plaza at 4949 East Lincoln Drive in Paradise Valley bordering Scottsdale.

Pepper Steak

1 1¾-pound filet mignon or New York strip steak	2 tablespoons oil
	2 tablespoons butter
Salt, to taste	¼ cup minced shallots
1 tablespoon green peppercorns	¾ cup Madeira wine
	¼ cup Armagnac or cognac.

Season the steak with salt and rub with the green peppercorns. Heat oil and butter in a deep skillet and sauté the steak in it 3 minutes on each side. Transfer steak to a hot serving dish and keep hot. Pour off the pan juice, add the shallots with Madeira wine and Armagnac to the skillet and scrape up all of the brown bits in the bottom of the pan. Heat and then flame. Bring to a boiling point, and reduce to half. Coat the steak with the sauce and serve very hot. Serves 4.

EL CHORRO LODGE

Scottsdale, Arizona • illustration by Mike Hagel

In operation since 1937, this desert hostelry has the old-time Spanish-Western atmosphere. Turn east off Black Canyon Freeway onto Glendale Avenue and drive about seven miles to 5550 East Lincoln Drive. Breakfast, lunch and dinner are served every day; overnight accommodations available. Reservations required. The lodge is open from October 1 through May. Hosts are Joe and Evie Miller.

Alaska King Crab Stroganoff

1 pound Alaska king crab meat	3 cups warm cream sauce
1 tablespoon butter	3 tablespoons ketchup
1 small onion, finely diced	2 teaspoons Worcestershire sauce
½ pound fresh mushrooms, sliced	4 tablespoons sour cream
¼ cup white wine	2 cups hot buttered noodles

Sauté onions and mushrooms in butter. Add crab meat in bite-size pieces when the onions are tender. Add wine and let simmer. Add cream sauce, ketchup and Worcestershire and simmer again to heat through. Fold in sour cream and heat. Pour over hot noodles. Serves 4.

Chocolate Ice Box Cake

Melt ½ pound of German's semisweet chocolate in top of a double boiler. Add 3 tablespoons water and blend before removing from heat. Add 4 egg yolks one at a time, beating vigorously until smooth and blended. Add 2 tablespoons confectioners' sugar and ½ cup chopped nuts. Beat 4 egg whites and 1 cup whipping cream; fold both into chocolate mixture. Line a dish with lady fingers and pour in mixture. Let set 12-24 hours in refrigerator. Serve topped with whipped cream.

THE TACK ROOM
Tucson, Arizona • illustration by Harry Borgman

Housed in the old and elegant Western-style hacienda called Rancho Del Rio, this resort-hotel dining room is one of the finest in the state. With special arrangements guests may order an exciting seven-course gourmet dinner. Only dinner is served. Reservations necessary for meals and for overnight accommodations. The resort is open every day, year-around; the dining room is closed Mondays from July 1 through October 1. It is at 2800 North Sabino Canyon Road and is owned by the Vactor and Kane families.

Steak Tartare

6 ounces finely chopped raw sirloin or tenderloin (no fat)	4 anchovy filets ⅛ tablespoon dry mustard

1 teaspoon red wine vinegar	1 tablespoon chopped parsley
1 tablespoon garlic oil	1 grated hard-boiled egg
2 dashes Tabasco sauce	Dash of cognac or brandy (optional)
2 dashes Worcestershire sauce	Salt and freshly ground pepper, to taste
1 raw egg yolk	
2 tablespoons minced onion	2 tablespoons capers

Reduce anchovy fillets to paste using 2 forks. Add mustard, vinegar, garlic oil, Tabasco and Worcestershire. Blend thoroughly and add egg yolk. Mix with meat. Add minced onion, parsley, grated egg, cognac, salt and pepper. Mix again and add capers. Serve on rye toast. Makes one portion.

WESTWARD LOOK RESORT
Tucson, Arizona • illustration by Fred Browning

Nestled in the foothills of the Santa Catalina Mountains, overlooking the city of Tucson, this luxurious resort spread out on 67 acres of the

105

Arizona desert is open year round as a total vacation spot or as a lunch or dinner stop. Recreational facilities include a golf course, tennis courts, swimming pool, riding horses and tours to historic locations. As traditional as the hospitality of the Southwest is here, so is the Continental cuisine offering guests gourmet meals prepared by a professional staff. Address is 245 East Ina Road, off I-10.

Veal Scaloppine, Gold Room

1 pound, 4 ounces top round veal	12 thin slices Italian prosciutto
Salt and pepper	2 cups heavy cream
½ cup flour	1 cup dry vermouth
½ cup clarified butter	

Slice veal into 12 slices, trim edges and pound between sheets of waxed paper until very thin. Season with salt and pepper. Dredge in flour and sauté in hot butter until lightly browned. Remove to hot platter. Sauté prosciutto quickly and place on top of veal. Remove excess butter from pan, add cream and vermouth. Cook until sauce is reduced and thick. Correct seasoning. Pour sauce over veal. Serve with fettucini. Serves 4.

THE KETTLE RESTAURANT
Anaheim, California • illustration by William Noonan

An Anaheim landmark, this restaurant features American cuisine and has an extensive seafood menu. Reservations necessary for lunch and dinner which are served weekdays. Closed Sunday and some holidays. From the Santa Ana Freeway, North, take the Lincoln Exit and proceed to 1776 West Lincoln.

Meat Loaf

Combine and mix well: 1½ pounds ground beef, 1½ cups stewed tomatoes (drained), ½ teaspoon pepper, 2 eggs, ⅛ teaspoon oregano, 1 teaspoon dried celery leaves, 1 medium onion (chopped fine), and 1 cup bread crumbs. Mold into loaf and top with 2 strips of bacon. Place in a pan and bake in 375° oven for about 1 hour. Serves 4-6.

Stuffed Pork Chops

Slit a pocket in 4 large, thick pork chops. Moisten 2 cups crumbled stale bread with water. To bread add: 1 cup cooked sausage meat, 1 small onion, chopped; pinch of sage, thyme, parsley and paprika. Season with salt and pepper. Blend stuffing, then fill pockets in chops. Place chops in baking pan and sprinkle with a teaspoon each of rosemary, parsley and paprika. Roast in 375° oven for 1 hour.

GULLIVER'S
Irvine, California • illustration by Neil Boyle

The 18th century world of Jonathan Swift is recreated here with the waitresses' costumes, antiques and hundreds of old *Gulliver's Travels* prints on the walls. Lunch is served Monday through Friday; dinner is served seven days a week. Reservations required. Take the MacArthur exit from the San Diego Freeway and go a half block to 18482 MacArthur Boulevard. It is 30 miles south of Los Angeles.

Corn au Gratin

Combine 1 pound of fresh or drained, canned whole kernel corn with 12 ounces of whipping cream and bring to a boil. With a slotted spoon seprate corn from the cream and return cream to fire. Make a paste from 1½ tablespoons of clear butter and

1½ tablespoons of flour combined, gradually add to cream to thicken. Simmer 5 minutes, then add 1 teaspoon salt, 2 tablespoons sugar and ½ teaspoon Ac'cent. Return corn to cream and bring back to a boil over low heat. Transfer creamed corn to a casserole, sprinkle top with 3 tablespoons Parmesan cheese and dot the top with melted butter. Brown under the broiler. Serves 4.

CHRISTIAN'S DANISH INN
La Mesa, California • illustration by Ben Eisenstat

A different menu featuring one main course is offered each day in this restaurant. Baked goods made on the premises and fresh vegetables are specialties. Reservations only. Guests should plan on a minimum of two hours for dinner. Closed on Sunday and Monday. It is 10 miles east of San Diego at 8235 University Avenue in La Mesa. Take the Spring Street exit from I-8, then turn east on University; it's just around the corner. Mr. and Mrs. Lewis Hansen are the owners.

Danish Liver Pâté

1 medium onion	¼ teaspoon pepper, or
2 cloves garlic	to taste
½ pound fatty bacon	¼ teaspoon ground
1 pound pork, lamb or	nutmeg
calf's liver	¼ teaspoon ground
3 large eggs	cloves
3½ tablespoons flour	2 tablespoons
1½ teaspoons salt, or to	Worcestershire sauce
taste	1 cup whipping cream

In a food processor fitted with a steel blade, combine onion, garlic and bacon until creamy and smooth. Put in a large mixing bowl. In the same unwashed processor bowl, purée the liver. Press the liver through a fine wire strainer into the bowl containing the bacon mixture. (This removes the tough membranes from the liver and saves time in trimming them.) Place all of the remaining ingredients in the bowl and blend thoroughly with an electric hand mixer. Pour into a pyrex loaf pan, 2½ x 4½ x 8½-inches, that has been liberally coated inside with lard. Place 2 or 3 bay leaves on top of liver. Cover the loaf pan tightly with aluminum foil greased with lard. Place loaf pan in a larger oven pan filled with water to ⅔ of the pâté pan. Bake in 325° oven for 1¼ hours or until the internal temperature is 160°. Remove pan from water, carefully taking off foil cover. Place a second loaf pan containing 3-4 pounds of weight on top of liver. Cool pâté while it is being pressed. When cool, slip pâté out of loaf pan, wrap in aluminum foil and refrigerate 3-4 hours. When firm, slice into ¼-inch slices.

BERMUDA INN REDUCING RESORT
Lancaster, California • illustration by Jan Cicala

A way to combine a vacation with weight loss is offered at this unique resort complex which serves only low calorie meals in its dining rooms. It is in the high desert country 65 miles north of Los Angeles. Take the Golden State Freeway to the Antelope Valley Freeway to Avenue "K" exit to 43019 Sierra Highway. It is open all year. Reservations necessary; dining room open only to registered guests.

House Dressing

1½ teaspoons	Few drops of sucaryl, to
McCormack's Season-all	taste
	1½ teaspoons celery
1 teaspoon sweet basil	seed
½ cup low calorie Italian	1½ teaspoons seasoned
dressing	pepper
1 cup dietetic tomato	
juice	

Blend all ingredients, refrigerate and shake well before using. Makes approximately 12 ounces — only 11 calories an ounce.

Vegetable Dip

¼ cup finely chopped
celery
½ tablespoon chopped
chives
2 small tomatoes, finely
chopped
½ carrot, shredded

¼ teaspoon
McCormack's Season-
all
Dash of ground pepper
Dash of Worcestershire
sauce

Combine first 4 ingredients. Add seasonings and mix well. Chill 3 hours. Serve with rye rounds or use as stuffing for whole boiled mushrooms. Makes 10 ounces (7 calories per ounce).

LARK CREEK INN
Larkspur, California • illustration by Neil Boyle

This delightful restaurant is in a lovely yellow and white 1888 Victorian house nestled under towering redwoods on the banks of Lark Creek. The inn serves lunch and dinner daily in the dining room and on a flower-filled patio when the weather permits. Closed Christmas Day. Take the Corte Madera turnoff from U.S. Highway 101, travel through the town to Magnolia, turn right and proceed one mile.

Baby Lobster Tails

16 Iceland frozen lobster
tails
Flour for dredging
4 tablespoons shallots
chopped very fine
8 tablespoons melted
butter, divided

½ cup California White
Riesling
4 teaspoons lemon juice
Salt and pepper
Chopped parsley, for
garnish

Peel the baby lobster tails, dip lightly in flour. Put 3 tablespoons butter in a skillet and sauté lobster tails. Add shallots, wine, lemon juice, salt and pepper and let simmer for about 4 minutes. Spoon remaining melted butter over the lobster tails. Remove quickly from pan. Place lobster tails in a serving dish, pour sauce over and sprinkle with chopped parsley. Serves 4.

LORD NELSON RESTAURANT
Long Beach, California • illustration by Neil Boyle

This unique dining room aboard the Queen Mary serves excellent food and affords diners a magnificent view of the bay and Long Beach skyline. Beautiful wood paneling, ship's lanterns and the unusual menu transport visitors to London. For a fee, guests may arrange guided tours of the entire ship. Lunch and dinner served daily. Take the Long Beach Freeway south to the very end. The ship is docked at Pier J in Long Beach. The Cambridge Garden Salade is tossed at the table as a friendly waitress tells what goes into it.

Cambridge Garden Salade

1 diced hard-cooked egg
½ cup cut raw
mushrooms
⅓ cup tiny cooked
shrimp
Bowl of chilled iceberg
and butter lettuce,
combined
Dressing
¾ cup mayonnaise
2 teaspoons Coleman's
dry mustard

5 tablespoons honey
1 cup salad oil
¼ cup white wine
vinegar
Dash of Worcestershire
sauce
Pinch of salt, pepper and
MSG
1 tablespoon chopped
parsley
1 tablespoon finely
chopped onion

Blend mayonnaise, mustard and honey. Add oil slowly, mixing constantly. Add remaining dressing ingredients. Blend well and chill one to two hours. Toss with salad, serve immediately.

WHALING STATION INN
Monterey, California • illustration by Robert Reynolds

This restaurant with an ambience reminiscent of the 1890s is in a quaint old building overlooking Cannery Row. John Pisto, the owner-chef, specializes in fresh seafood, steaks and Italian dishes. California wines are featured; French wines are also available. Dinner served daily 5:30 to 10:30 p.m. Reservations advisable. The address is 763 Wave Street.

Clams and Linguine

Put ⅛ cup olive oil, ¼ pound butter and several chopped cloves of garlic in each of two large heavy frying pans. Sauté until garlic is opaque. Add 64-96 clams (8-12 per serving). Sprinkle each pan with freshly ground pepper, ½ cup chopped parsley and 2-4 cups of clam juice. Cover and steam clams open (6 to 10 minutes). Broth should have a rich yellow look — add more butter if necessary. Drain 2 pounds cooked linguine, place in deep dishes. Place clams on top of pasta, then pour broth over all. Top with freshly grated Parmesan cheese. Serves 8.

Hot Spicy Scallops

In a large, heavy frying pan, place 1 tablespoon butter and ⅛ cup peanut oil. Sauté lightly 3 cloves chopped garlic, 1 large onion (diced), ½ green pepper (slivered) and 2-inch piece of ginger (crushed). Add 80-96 fresh, plump scallops (10-12 per person), ½ cup dry sherry and 1 tablespoon fish sauce (available at Oriental food stores). Add ground red pepper or hot chili, to taste. Thicken with tablespoon of cornstarch. Cook scallops until tender. Serve. Makes 8 portions.

THE JACKS' DEER CREEK PLAZA
Nevada City, California • illustration by Wilfrid Duehren

Jack Beggs and Jack Wentz bought and restored this historic 115-year-old building, which has five interesting dining rooms and one outdoor dining deck. In northern California, it is 63 miles north of Sacramento and an hour's drive from Lake Tahoe. Lunch (11:30 to 2) and dinner (6 to 9) served daily except Tuesday and Sunday; dinner only on Sunday (6 to 9). Closed Tuesday and from December 21 through 26. Reservations advisable. The address is 101 Broad Street. Take State Highway 49 from I-80.

Cream of Avocado Soup

Melt ¼ cup of butter, stir in 2 tablespoons of flour. Make a smooth paste and heat over low fire, slowly add 2 quarts of rich, seasoned chicken stock and stir until mixture is smooth and thick. In a blender puree 4 ripe, peeled avocados with 1 cup of milk. Season with salt, pepper and dash of curry powder. Add avocado to chicken stock and let simmer for 10 minutes. Chill. Serves 8.

ALDO'S
Sacramento, California • illustration by Art Riley

The two owners are vitally involved in this elegant restaurant's daily operations. Aldo Bovero is the charming host who greets guests, and Paul Coulat is the executive chef who supervises the preparation of the Continental dishes that have made this establishment justly famous. Open daily for lunch and dinner. Closed Sunday. Reservations advisable. It is at 2914-16 Pasatiempo Lane.

Coquilles Saint-Jacques

Melt 4 tablespoons butter in a sauce pan. When hot, add 1 teaspoon chopped shallots. Sauté a

few minutes but do not allow to brown. Add 1 pound quartered scallops, ¼ pound peeled, deveined and quartered prawns and ½ pound Dungeness crab legs. Sauté a few minutes. Add 1½ cups dry white wine and a few drops of lemon juice.

In a separate pan, sauté ¾ pound of mushrooms that have been quartered. Add to seafood mixture. Place in casserole and bake in 350° oven for 15 minutes until scallops and prawns are cooked. Melt 4 tablespoons butter in sauce pan, add 5 tablespoons flour gradually, stirring constantly. Do not brown. Add ¾ cup milk, a small amount at a time, stirring constantly until mixture begins to thicken. Drain excess fish liquid and reduce liquid to one cup, then add to flour mixture. Let simmer slowly for about 3 minutes. Mix 2 egg yolks with ½ cup whipping cream and stir into sauce. Add 1 teaspoon salt and ½ teaspoon white pepper. Pour over scallops, prawns and crab legs, stirring carefully. Place in 6 scallop shells or ramekins and sprinkle with ⅓ cup Parmesan cheese. Bake 15 minutes at 450°. Scallop shell can be garnished with whipped potato border. Serves 6.

THE STEINBECK HOUSE

Salinas, California • illustration by Robert Boston

Dining at the large, gray frame house where John Steinbeck was born in 1902 is a unique experience. It is a gourmet luncheon spot at 132 Central Avenue operated by Valley Guild, a nonprofit organization whose purpose is to maintain and preserve the Nobel Prize winner's home. The restaurant is open for lunch, Monday through Friday, by reservation only. The chef-manager is Dee McAvary. There are two sittings, at 11:45 a.m. and 1:15 p.m.

Elegant Chocolate Cheese Cake

In a blender combine: 4 eggs, 1½ cups sugar, 6 tablespoons cocoa, 1 teaspoon vanilla and 8 ounces of cream cheese. Cover and blend until smooth; pour half the mixture into a bowl, then add another 8 ounces of cream cheese to the blender jar, and blend until smooth. Stir 4 cups of sour cream into mixture in the bowl, then blend in remaining cheese mixture from blender. (If using a mixer, beat cheese until smooth, mix in sugar, cocoa, vanilla and eggs, one at a time, then add the sour cream.) Pour chocolate batter into chocolate crust (below) in a cheese cake pan (spring form). Bake in 350° oven for 1 hour and 20 minutes or until edge is set and dull in color, while the 4-inch center diameter is glossy looking. When cool, remove pan rim and set cake on a serving dish. Pile cream topping (below) in the center of the cake. Grate semisweet chocolate over cream.

Chocolate Crust

In a 9-inch spring form pan, blend 2 cups finely crushed chocolate wafer cookie crumbs with ¼ cup sugar, ¼ teaspoon cinnamon and 7 tablespoons melted butter. With a spoon, press crumbs over bottom and 3 inches up the sides.

Cream Topping

In a small electric mixer bowl, cream 3 ounces cream cheese until soft. Gradually add ½ cup whipping cream. Mix at high speed to the consistency of stiffly whipped cream. Blend in ¼ cup powdered sugar and 1 tablespoon crème de cacao or a coffee flavored liqueur. Cover and chill until ready to use.

Creamy Lettuce Soup

In a 2-quart sauce pan heat 2 tablespoons butter. Add 1 small chopped onion, sauté until soft. Stir in 2 tablespoons flour, ½ teaspoon salt and ⅛ teaspoon pepper. Blend and cook until bubbly. Gradually add 2 cans (10½-ounce) of beef broth to onion mixture. Heat slowly, stir in 2 cups half-and-half cream. Reheat to just below boiling. Shred ¼ head iceberg lettuce — cut across at 1-inch intervals — to make bite size. Put about ¼ cup lettuce in each bowl, ladle hot soup over lettuce and garnish with grated nutmeg or chopped parsley. Serves 6.

SAN CLEMENTE INN

San Clemente, California • illustration by Larry Murtry

Located midway between Los Angeles and San Diego, this delightful inn offers visitors access to all of the major attractions of two metropolitan areas within an hour's drive. The main dining room opens onto a glass-enclosed sun balcony overlooking the Pacific. Breakfast, lunch and dinner served; overnight accommodations. Reservations advised. The address is 125 Avenida Esplandian.

Chicken Jerusalem

Wash and disjoint a 3½-pound frying chicken, discarding ribs and as many bones as possible. Cut off wing tips and leg knuckles. Salt and pepper lightly. In a sauté pan, add 3 tablespoons oil or clarified butter and place on medium heat. When oil is hot, place chicken pieces, skin side down, in pan and let fry until golden brown, about 10-15 minutes. Add 8 medium-size raw mushroom caps, turn chicken over and cook for 5-6 minutes. Add 1 tablespoon finely chopped onion and 1 teaspoon chopped garlic or shallot. Shake pan so that onion and shallot will be in oil. When chicken is light brown on both sides, drain oil and add 1 cup dry Sauterne or Chablis. Let simmer with cover on until wine is almost completely reduced. Add enough rich cream sauce, about 2 cups, to cover chicken. Add 1 tablespoon sliced water chestnuts and 6 small canned artichoke hearts. Simmer for 5 minutes. Serve with 4 cups hot buttered rice or spaghetti. Top chicken with 2 tablespoons salted, toasted almonds. Makes 4 portions.

THE BRIGANTINE

San Diego, California • illustration by Bud Shackelford

Great seafood served in a cozy nautical atmosphere has made this restaurant justly famous. One of the most popular dishes is "Cioppino," a California contribution to great seafood dishes. Dinner is served every night; lunch served Monday through Friday. The address is 2912 Shelter Island Drive.

Cioppino

Sauté the following in ½ cup of olive oil: 1¼ medium onions, chopped; 1 stalk celery, chopped; 4 cloves garlic, crushed or minced; and 2 tablespoons fresh chopped parsley or 1½ teaspoons dry parsley flakes. When vegetables are soft, add 3½ tablespoons red wine vinegar; ¾ cup burgundy wine; 1½ teaspoons allspice; 1 tablespoon salt, 2 cups water, 1 No. 303 can of tomato sauce and 1 No. 303 can of stewed tomatoes. Then add a quart of fish stock and simmer for 1½ hours until mixture thickens.

Divide the following seafood equally into 6 individual ovenproof casseroles (with covers) or one large oven casserole: 1 pound fresh or frozen raw cleaned shrimp, 12 ounces fresh or frozen scallops, 12 scrubbed raw clams, 1 pound King or Dungeness crab legs, cracked; 1 pound boned whitefish, cut in chunks; and 6 lemon wedges. Fill casseroles to the brim with sauce, cover and bake in preheated 450° oven for 20 to 30 minutes. Provide bowls for discarding bones and shells. Serve with hot sourdough bread. Makes 6 generous portions.

CHEZ MARGUERITE

San Francisco, California • illustration by Robert Lydecker

The famous Powell Street cable car passes directly in front of this restaurant. Housed in an ornate Victorian building, the small, candle-lit dining room is pure Paris bistro. Dinner served daily, Wednesday through Sunday; closed Monday and Tuesday. Owners Herb Emery and Ross Williams suggest reservations. In San Francisco's North Beach area, it is at 2330 Taylor.

Belgian Hare Bruxelloise

4 hares or rabbits, each 2½ pounds	2 leeks, sliced
Salt and pepper	½ pound rendered salt pork, cut into finger length strips
1 teaspoon powdered thyme	½ cup wine vinegar
2 cloves garlic, minced	4 cups (or more) red wine
3 tablespoons flour	
4 tablespoons cooking fat	2 ounces butter
2 onions, sliced	10 cooked pearl onions
	10 mushroom caps

Cut hares into serving pieces. Season with salt, pepper, thyme, and minced garlic. Dredge the hare lightly in flour, then sauté in hot fat until lightly browned. Add onions, leeks, salt pork, wine vinegar and enough good red wine to cover. Cook over medium flame for ¾ hour, then skim off fat. Add the butter mixed with enough flour to make a medium thick sauce (about 3 tablespoons). Serve hot in individual oval shaped casseroles with a garnish of cooked pearl onions (which have been sautéed in butter until brown, sprinkled with sugar and simmered until tender in a few spoonfuls of red wine) and mushroom caps (sautéed in butter with a clove of garlic). Serves 8-10.

Tripe à la Creole

Cut 3 pounds honeycomb tripe in 2-inch pieces and boil for 15 minutes in salted water. Set aside to drain. Sauté in heavy skillet with 3 tablespoons of oil: 1 large sliced onion; 2 large sliced carrots and 1 large bell pepper, cut into 1-inch pieces. Sauté for 5-15 minutes. Add: ½ cup tomato puree; 1 cup stewed tomatoes; 2 cups dry white wine; 1 cup beef stock or bouillon; 1 bay leaf; 1 clove crushed garlic; 1 tablespoon salt; ½ teaspoon fine black pepper; 4 dashes Tabasco sauce and ¼ teaspoon thyme. Add tripe to skillet and simmer ingredients approximately 5 minutes. Pour skillet contents into covered casserole. Bake in preheated 375° oven for 2½ to 3 hours. Serves 6.

FOURNOU'S OVENS

San Francisco, California • illustration by Mike Gawet

This unique restaurant's massive tile-faced open-hearth ovens produce roasts of every description, served with accompaniments of Continental cuisine and offerings from an extensive wine cellar. The restaurant is on the first level of the elegant Stanford Court Hotel on Nob Hill at the corner of California and Powell Streets where San Francisco's cable car lines cross. Dinner served every night from 6 to 11 p.m. Reservations necessary for both dinner and hotel accommodations.

Roast Duckling with Green Peppercorns and Kumquat Sauce

3 ducks (about 4-5 pounds each), dressed	6 carrots, peeled, sliced
	Salt, pepper to taste
1 large onion, coarsely chopped	1 quart box fresh kumquats
2 stalks celery, cut in 1-inch slices	¼ cup vinegar

½ pound sugar,
 granulated
1 cup fresh orange juice
¼ cup fresh lemon juice
½ teaspoon crushed
 black peppercorns
1 bay leaf
1 small sprig thyme

1 small leek, sliced fine
1 pint demi-glaze (brown
 sauce)
½ cup tomato paste
1 jigger Cointreau or
 Grand Marnier
2 tablespoons green
 peppercorns

Wipe and dry ducks. Divide onion, celery and carrots in thirds and fill each duck cavity with the vegetables. Sprinkle with salt, pepper. Roast ducks at 425° for 45 minutes on rack to allow fat to drain off. Peel half of the kumquats, removing all pulp from peel. Cut peels in fine julienne, cover with boiling water for 1 minute, drain and reserve. In a sauce pan over medium heat, cook vinegar and sugar until it begins to caramelize. Add orange and lemon juice and the pulp from peeled kumquats. Cook till liquid reduces about one-fourth. Add the kumquat julienne, crushed peppercorns, bay leaf, thyme and leek. Simmer until golden brown. Then add the demi-glaze (brown sauce) and tomato paste. Simmer, stirring occasionally, for one hour. Strain through a fine sieve and add the liqueur and whole green peppercorns. Drain all juices and fat from roasted ducks, halve them and arrange on heated platters. Garnish with remaining kumquats cut in thin slices. Reheat and serve sauce separately. Serves 6.

Praline Ice Cream Pie

Heat ½ cup brown sugar until it reaches the point where it begins to turn darker. Mix with ½ cup whipping cream and 1 ounce melted butter. Add 4 ounces crushed pecans and 2 teaspoons vanilla. In a separate bowl whip 1½ quarts of vanilla ice cream, and then mix until well blended with the brown sugar mixture (praline). Place this mixture in a deep 9-inch, baked pie shell and top with meringue. Brown quickly under broiler.

MacARTHUR PARK
San Francisco, California • illustration by Norman Nicholson

High arched windows of an old warehouse were opened to ground level for entranceways. Inside, separate dining rooms are formed by screens of greenery backed by a garden and enclosed aviary. Dinner served Monday through Thursday 5:30 to 10:30 p.m., Friday and Saturday until 11:30 p.m. On Sunday, brunch 10:30 a.m. to 2:30 p.m. and dinner 5 to 10 p.m. The address is 607 Front Street between Jackson and Pacific.

Onion Soup

6 medium onions, sliced
1 tablespoon olive oil
¼ pound butter
½ teaspoon black
 pepper
1½ teaspoons salt
1 teaspoon sugar
½ teaspoon thyme
4 bay leaves
1 clove garlic, diced

1 teaspoon caraway
 seeds
2 tablespoons Lea &
 Perrins steak sauce
2 quarts beef stock
½ cup dry white wine
24-30 buttered croutons
½ cup grated Parmesan
 cheese
8-10 slices Swiss cheese

In a large soup pot, sauté onions in butter and olive oil. Brown well. Add all seasonings and steak sauce to onions. Simmer over low heat for 10 minutes. Add beef stock and boil 1 hour. Add wine. Boil 10 minutes. Place 3 croutons in each of 8 oven-proof soup bowls. Sprinkle with Parmesan cheese. Pour in soup, top with Swiss cheese. Bake in 350° oven until brown.

NORTH BEACH RESTAURANT
San Francisco, California • illustration by Marc Gobé

Lorenzo Petroni is the genial host and owner of this delightful restaurant. Mr. Petroni frequently serves customers with fish caught from his own fishing boat. And he personally prepares the restaurant's outstanding Buon Gusto salami. Lunch and dinner served daily; reservations necessary. Closed most holidays. The address is 1512 Stockton in the North Beach area of San Francisco.

Cioppino

6 pounds mixed seafood
 shrimp, crab, lobster,
 calamari (squid), filet
 of sole, mussels and
 clams
½ cup olive oil

2 cups onion, finely
 chopped
1 cup celery, finely
 chopped
2 cloves garlic, minced
 or mashed
1 tablespoon salt

113

1 teaspoon pepper
1 tablespoon each:
   oregano, fresh
   rosemary and
   marjoram

1 can (1 pound, 13
   ounces) solid-pack
   tomatoes
2 cups dry white wine

Clean and cut calamari into slices, shell and devein shrimp, clean mussel and clam shells. Cut lobster and crab into serving pieces. Heat olive oil and add onion, celery, garlic and seasonings. Cook for five minutes then add tomatoes which have been peeled, seeded and coarsely chopped. Add seafood, except clams and mussels. Add wine. Cover pot and simmer until almost done, about 30 minutes. Add clams and mussels, cover pot and simmer about 10 minutes more or until shells open. Serve in big bowls over slices of toasted French bread. Makes 6-8 portions.

PAPRIKAS FONO

San Francisco, California • illustration by William E. Paull

Laszlo and Paulette Fono, originators of the famous Magic Pan crêperies, have opened this authentic Hungarian restaurant in Ghiradelli Square. Diners can either sit inside at tables around a huge copper kettle from which gulyas — a meal-in-itself herdsman's soup — is served, or enjoy their fare on a glassed-in balcony that provides a spectacular view of the square below and the bay in the distance. Luncheon from 11:30 a.m. to 5:30 p.m.; dinner served 5:30 to 11 p.m., every day. Reservations suggested. The address is 900 North Point.

Veal Paprikás

Dice 3 medium onions and sauté in 5 tablespoons of oil for 5 minutes over low heat in a heavy 5-quart casserole with a tight fitting lid. Stir frequently until the onions are golden. Take casserole off heat, add 3 tablespoons Hungarian paprika and mix well. Place 3 pounds of leg of veal (cut into one-inch cubes) on top of paprika mixture. Turn pieces to coat them well. Cook over low heat for a few minutes, stirring continuously so the paprika does not burn. Add 2 teaspoons salt, ½ teaspoon white pepper, 1½ cups of water and 1 large green pepper. Cook, uncovered, over low heat for 35 minutes. Taste for seasoning, remove green pepper and discard. Test veal for tenderness — do not overcook as meat will fall apart. Mix ½ cup sour cream with 1 rounded tablespoon flour and 1 tablespoon cold water in a separate bowl. Add 1 tablespoon paprika sauce from the cooked meat to the sour cream. Mix well. Add this to the sauce in the pot. Serve immediately with galuska (below). Makes 6 portions.

Galuska (Egg Dumplings)

Combine 3 cups of flour with 1 tablespoon of salt in a large mixing bowl. Mix well with a wooden spoon. Add 3 whole eggs and 1 cup of water. Beat with spoon for 2 minutes or until there are no large lumps of egg and flour. Scrape sides of the bowl. Pour a teaspoon of oil over dough to prevent it from drying. Bring 3 quarts of water to boil in a large pot, add 1 tablespoon of salt. Take a small cutting board and place ⅓ of the dough on it. Dip knife into boiling water and then cut a narrow (about ¼ inch wide) strip of dough. Lean the cutting board over the top of the pot, and cut quickly, with a cutting and scraping motion, scraping the dough off the board into the water. Dip the knife frequently into the boiling water. When dumplings float to the top, allow to boil briefly. Stir and remove dumplings with a strainer. Quickly wash with cold water. Place in a casserole. Dribble 4 tablespoons melted butter over galuska. Repeat until all dough is used. Mix thoroughly so all galuska is coated with butter.

THE CAPISTRANO DEPOT
San Juan Capistrano, California • illustration by Neil Boyle

The heart of this restaurant is a restored 1895 depot. On tracks around the station are nine railroad cars (including a 1927 Pullman), which are used for dining and banquet rooms. Open every day for lunch and dinner; Sunday brunch served. Reservations advisable. It is near the 1776 mission of San Juan Capistrano at 26701 Verdugo Street.

Mustard Eggs

4 cups Mornay sauce (cream sauce made with cheese)	16 hard-boiled eggs
2 tablespoons dry mustard	32 slices fried bacon
	Toast points

Mix dry mustard with a little water and beat with a whip until smooth. Stir this into hot Mornay sauce until well mixed. Slice hard-boiled eggs and arrange in a large casserole or 8 individual ones. Cover with mustard sauce and place bacon slices on top. Put in 350° oven for 5 minutes and serve with hot toast points. Makes 8 portions.

CASTAGNOLA'S
Santa Cruz, California • illustration by Lou McMurray

Overlooking the San Lorenzo River and a city park in downtown Santa Cruz, this popular restaurant is at 119 River Street, South. Lunch served Tuesday through Friday; dinner Tuesday through Sunday; closed Monday. Reservations necessary.

Veal Carmody

12 veal scallops (¼-inch thick, 2 to 3 inches in diameter)	⅓ cup olive oil
½ cup flour	3 cups fresh sliced mushrooms

¾ cup chopped green onions	½ teaspoon white pepper
1 teaspoon salt	1 tablespoon sweet basil
1 tablespoon garlic powder	1½ cups dry sherry
	1½ cups quartered artichoke hearts

Flatten veal pieces, dredge in flour, then sauté in hot oil until lightly browned. Drain off oil from skillet. Add mushrooms, green onions, salt, garlic powder, pepper and basil. Sauté 3 to 5 minutes. Add sherry and cook over medium heat about 8 minutes. Stir in artichokes and heat gently. Serves 4.

HORSELESS CARRIAGE
Sepulveda, California • illustration by Neil Boyle

Celebrating its 12th anniversary, this unique restaurant caters to the entire range of tastes—whether it be for a simple breakfast or a complete lobster dinner. The restaurant is owned by and is part of a Ford dealership, Galpin Ford. Breakfast, lunch and dinner served every day. Take the Roscoe Boulevard exit ramp from the San Diego Freeway to 15505 Roscoe Boulevard, a block east.

Baked Cod Bella Vista

3½ pounds fresh cod · 1 green pepper
2 chopped shallots · 1 medium onion
4 tablespoons butter · 8 slices tomato
¼ cup white wine · Salt to taste

Cut cod in 7-ounce portions. Sauté chopped shallots in butter, add wine and cod. Cut green pepper and onion into 8 slices and place a slice of each on top of fish pieces. Add tomato slices overlapping on top of fish. Cover with greased brown paper. Bake at 375° for 15 to 20 minutes. Remove cover and baste cod after the first 10 minutes. Add salt to taste. Serves 8.

AU RELAIS
Sonoma, California • illustration by John Nicolini

Harold and Dorothy Marsden remodeled an old Victorian home at 691 Broadway in downtown Sonoma. French windows open onto a garden patio for alfresco dining. French country cuisine lovingly prepared by chef-owner Marsden has won a discerning clientele. Lunch and dinner served daily; closed Tuesday. Reservations advisable.

Poulet Sauté

Cut two boned chicken breasts into pieces and flatten with a cleaver. Dredge them in seasoned flour. Sauté the filets lightly in 2 tablespoons each of butter and olive oil about 8 minutes on each side, or until lightly browned. Remove chicken from pan. Deglaze pan with ¼ cup of dry sherry. In another pan sauté together ½ pound of bacon cut into cubes and 1½ pounds of whole mushrooms. Drain off excess bacon fat. Return chicken to original pan with sherry; add drained bacon, mushrooms and 24 tiny parboiled onions. Cover pan and simmer for about 8 minutes. Divide 2 cups of hot buttered rice into 4 portions, then divide chicken dish and place over rice. Serves 4.

GINO'S OF SONOMA
Sonoma, California • illustration by Norman Nicholson

This small and attractively designed restaurant features authentic Italian food served piping hot from an immaculate kitchen. The recipes come from the Marche region of Italy. Lunch only, 11 a.m. to 2:30 p.m. (no dinners). It is at 422 First Street East, on the plaza in Sonoma.

Chicken Montpellier

2½ pounds skinned chicken thighs, legs and breasts · 1 can black olives (6 ounces)
¾ cup oil · 6 large tomatoes, peeled and cut into pieces
3 onions, chopped · 2 green peppers, cut into bite size pieces
3 cloves garlic, chopped · ¼ teaspoon each: thyme, basil and parsley
1¼ teaspoons paprika
Salt and pepper, to taste

Heat oil, add chicken pieces and sauté for a few minutes. Add onions, garlic, paprika, salt and pepper. Cook until onion is lightly browned; add tomatoes, peppers, herbs and olives. Simmer 1 hour or until chicken is done. Serves 4.

BOCCACCIO'S
Westlake Village, California • illustration by Neil Boyle

This popular and attractive restaurant is situated on the edge of a 150-acre lake in Westlake Village, a planned country-community near Los Angeles where golf, tennis, riding and sailing are available to visitors. One can dine under dim lights in a romantic atmosphere, or take lunch on the patio from which a view of the sailboats on the lake is spectacular. The restaurant is open year-round, and lunch and dinner are served every day except Monday. The address is 32123 Lindero Canyon Road; take Lindero Canyon

exit from U.S. Highway 101 and follow directions for six blocks to "The Landing" on the lake. Reservations are advisable for dinner.

Steak au Poivre

4 10-ounce sirloin steaks
Salt and freshly crushed
   peppercorns
4 ounces butter

4 ounces white wine
8 ounces brown sauce
2 ounces Lea & Perrins
   sauce

Salt both sides of steaks. Then lay in bed of crushed pepper and turn. Brown peppered steaks on both sides in butter. Dispose of drippings and remove steaks from pan. Add wine and reduce; add butter, brown sauce, Lea & Perrins sauce and salt to taste. Place steaks on plates and pour sauce over steaks. Makes 4 servings.

MAGNOLIA HOTEL
Yountville, California • illustration by Gilbert DiCicco

Fifty-five miles north of San Francisco, this delightful 106-year-old hotel — owned and operated by Bruce and Bonnie Locken — is in the heart of the Napa Valley wine country. Each of the hotel's 10 rooms is furnished with antiques, and provided with a decanter of port wine. There is a Jacuzzi-type spa and a heated swimming pool. Dinner, with an extensive wine list, is served to non-guests Thursday through Sunday; reservations necessary. The hotel is open every day. The address is 6529 Young Street.

French Toast with Port Wine Syrup

6 slices white or French
   bread
1 cup half and half
6 eggs

1 tablespoon vanilla
½ teaspoon cinnamon
Butter
Powdered sugar

Whip together the half and half, eggs, vanilla and cinnamon. Dip bread slices in mixture. Fry in plenty of butter until well browned on both sides. Sprinkle with powdered sugar and serve with hot Port Wine Syrup (below).

Port Wine Syrup

½ cup water
1½ cups sugar

½ cup port wine

Combine water and sugar, bring to boiling. Add wine and bring again to boiling. Store unused syrup in refrigerator.

FLAGSTAFF HOUSE
Boulder, Colorado • illustration by James Stelma

A picturesque dining spot on the side of a mountain, on Flagstaff Mountain Road, this restaurant is a little over a mile west of the city of Boulder. It offers a magnificent view of the city and of the Colorado plains. Dinner is served every day; reservations recommended. Don Monette is the owner.

King Crab Lausanne

Layer in a casserole 4 pounds King Crab meat pieces, 8 large fresh mushrooms and 8 canned artichoke hearts. Make a sauce by combining 3 cups rich fish stock (or 13-ounce can crab bisque with 3 cups water), 3 cups heavy cream, 2 teaspoons Dijon mustard, 2 teaspoons curry powder, ½ cup white wine and salt and pepper, to taste. Make a roux by melting 4 tablespoons butter and mixing with 4 tablespoons flour until it forms a smooth paste. Stir this into sauce and cook together, stirring constantly until sauce thickens slightly. Pour over casserole and bake for 10 minutes at 375° in a preheated oven. Serves 8-10.

Honey Mustard Dressing

4 cups mayonnaise
2 cups prepared mustard
2 cups honey
1 cup creamy Italian dressing

Blend ingredients well and serve on fresh spinach or tossed green salad with sliced fresh mushrooms, bean sprouts, bacon bits and shredded hard-boiled eggs. Store extra dressing in refrigerator. Makes 2 quarts.

GREENBRIAR INN
Boulder, Colorado • illustration by Mike Hagel

It's hard to recognize this charming restaurant as the country store and gas station it was 10 years ago, before Rudi Zwicker set out to remodel. Located at the base of the Rockies, it is open for dinner, by reservation, year round with noon servings on holidays. The extensive menu ranges from mountain trout, seafoods and Continental favorites to steaks and roasts, with a large wine selection. Address, Route 36, Left Hand Canyon, 8 miles north of Boulder.

Filet of Beef Wellington

1½ pounds center cut filet of beef
Butter, salt, pepper
1 cup liver pâté
¼ cup chopped mushrooms
2 tablespoons Madeira
Puff pastry (for shortcut, use frozen prepared pastry)
2 egg yolks, beaten

Rub beef with butter, sprinkle with salt and pepper. Place on rack and roast at 450° to 120 degrees (very rare) on thermometer, about 20 minutes. Remove from oven and cool thoroughly. Beat pâté, mushrooms and Madeira until smooth. Spread evenly over cooled filet, including bottom. Roll pastry ¼-inch thick to fit over and around filet. Place filet on pastry, overlapping edges to form a seam. Moisten edges to seal and place on baking pan, seam side down. Brush with egg yolk. Bake at 425° 10 minutes; reduce to 375° and bake 15 to 20 minutes or until evenly browned. Let rest 10 minutes in warm place before carving. Serves 4.

THE GREAT AMERICAN WINERY
Pueblo, Colorado • illustration by Robert Boston

There are four small dining rooms, each with its own fireplace, in this interesting restaurant owned by Douglas Ring. His wine cellar is one of the best-stocked in the West. Just a few miles from Pueblo Dam and Lake, it is four blocks north of U.S. Highway 50, at 4289 North Elizabeth Street, which runs parallel to I-25. Dinner is served every day, except Sunday and major holidays. Reservations not taken.

Garlic Steak with Mushroom Sauce

Rub 4 12-ounce top sirloin steaks with garlic puree. Place in cast iron skillet with ½ pound of melted butter, remaining garlic salt and 1 bunch green onions, finely chopped. Cook 10 minutes in garlic butter, over low to medium heat, turning steaks often. Transfer steaks to a greased cast iron skillet. Allow garlic butter to continue cooking over low heat while steaks are being finished. Transfer steaks to serving plates and top with mushroom sauce (below). Serves 4.

Mushroom Sauce

Add 1 pound of fresh sliced mushrooms to 1 cup of melted butter. Sauté for a few minutes, then add a dash of dry vermouth, 1 teaspoon fresh lemon juice and 1 teaspoon of garlic puree. Cook a few more minutes and serve hot on garlic steaks. Sauce also can be served on broiled beef patties.

THE PEPPER MILL

Snowmass, Colorado • illustration by Georgeann Waggamen

Ruth and Bob Kevan are the principal owners and operators of this charming restaurant decorated with antique stained glass windows and hanging plants. Dinner is served every day. Turn off State Highway 82 and follow Brush Creek Road to the Mall at Snowmass. Closed mid-April to June 15 and October through Thanksgiving. Reservations necessary.

Rigatoni with Cheese

Prepare sauce by browning 1 pound ground beef with 1 chopped onion and a clove of garlic, minced. Pour off fat. Add 4 cups well-seasoned spaghetti sauce. Simmer slowly, the longer the better, but at least 30 minutes. Boil 8 ounces of rigatoni noodles (slightly underdone). In a buttered casserole dish, layer the rigatoni noodles with ¼ pound sliced provolone cheese. Spread ¾ cup of sour cream over provolone and top with half of the sauce. Add another layer of noodles, a layer of ¼ pound sliced Mozzarella and the remainder of the sauce. Sprinkle generously with grated Parmesan cheese. Bake uncovered at 350° for 30 minutes. Serves 4.

BRANDYWINE

Steamboat Springs, Colorado • illustraion by Georgeann Waggaman

Antiques and handcrafted stained glass windows are distinctive aspects of the decor at this fine eating place in the area of Mt. Werner Ski Resort and Cliff Buchholz's Tennis Ranch. Lunch and dinner are served every day; reservations not accepted. The address is 57½ 8th Street in downtown Steamboat Springs. Tom Watson is the manager.

Ratatouille with Sausage

3 cloves garlic, finely
  minced
2 onions, thinly sliced
⅓ cup olive oil
1 green pepper, cut into
  thin rounds
2 medium eggplants,
  diced and unpeeled
2 medium zucchini,
  sliced ¼-inch thick
1 20-ounce can whole
  Italian tomatoes
1½ teaspoons basil
1½ teaspoons parsley
1½ teaspoons salt
Freshly ground pepper,
  to taste
1½ pounds Italian
  sausage, sliced
½ pound whole
  mushrooms
1 cup grated Swiss
  cheese

Sauté garlic and onions in oil until soft. Add green pepper, eggplant and zucchini and cook 5 minutes over medium heat, tossing well. Add tomatoes with liquid and seasonings. Simmer 30 minutes, covered for last half of the time. Meanwhile cook sausage in frying pan until done and drain well. Add mushrooms to vegtables during last 10 minutes of cooking time. Add sausage to vegetables. Sprinkle with grated cheese. Cover and simmer until cheese melts. Serves 8.

CANLIS RESTAURANT
Honolulu, Hawaii • illustration by Frederick Browning

A wall of orchids greets visitors at the entrance to this spectacularly beautiful restaurant located in the heart of Waikiki. Open for dinner every day from 5 p.m. to 2 a.m.; reservations advisable. Closed Labor Day, Thanksgiving and Christmas. Drive toward Diamond Head on Nimitz to Ala Moana to 2100 Kalakaua where the restaurant is located. Peter Canlis is the owner of this 30-year-old restaurant.

Canlis Shrimp

2 pounds large shrimp, shelled (except tail)	¼ teaspoon salt
1 ounce olive oil	¼ teaspoon freshly ground black pepper
1 ounce butter	2 lemons (juice only)
1 small garlic clove, crushed	2 ounces dry vermouth

Place olive oil in a large skillet. Heat; when it simmers add shrimp and allow to cook until golden brown. Reduce heat, add butter, garlic, salt and pepper. When you think you have too much salt add more. When well blended turn fire to very hot. Add lemon juice and dry vermouth and cook for about 1 minute, constantly stirring or shaking. Serves 8 as an appetizer or entree.

ROBAIRE'S FRENCH RESTAURANT
Kihei, Maui, Hawaii • illustration by Vern Tremewen

The beauty of the setting is equaled only by the excellence of the cuisine in this delightful and intimate French restaurant owned and operated by Robert Goueytes and his Hawaiian wife, Lee. Many of the menu favorites are transplants from Robert's native home in the south of France. His skill as chef shows in the way he combines native Hawaiian foods with French cooking methods. Open for dinner,

reservations suggested, Tuesday to Saturday from April to the middle of December, then Monday through Saturday. Closed the month of June. Address 61 South Kihei Road off Highway 31.

Opakapaka Robaire (Boneless Filets of Island Fish)

2 pounds red snapper filets	2 tablespoons chopped fresh shrimp
1 cup flour	1 tablespoon chopped parsley
2 tablespoons butter	2 cups white wine
6 fresh mushrooms, sliced	1 cup heavy cream
1 teaspoon chopped shallots	Salt to taste
	Chopped parsley

Dredge fish with flour. Heat butter in large skillet. Add filets and sauté until lightly browned on both sides. Remove fish to shallow baking pan. Add mushrooms, shallots, shrimp and parsley to pan. Cook and stir 2 minutes. Add wine, stir and cook until reduced by half. Stir in cream. Pour over fish and bake in pre-heated 350° oven 10 to 15 minutes or until sauce is bubbly. Salt to taste. Garnish with chopped parsley. Serves 4.

COCONUT PALACE DINING ROOM
Lihue, Hawaii • illustration by Larry McManus

One of the dining rooms at Coco Palms Resort, on the Hawaiian island of Kauai, it is nestled between a lazy, water-lily fringed lagoon and the edge of a historic 2,000 palm grove. Dinner served daily; complete resort facilities. Reservations necessary for meals and for overnight accommodations. Mrs. Grace Guslander, a noted authority on Hawaiian food and customs, is the manager.

Kupa He'i Maka (Green Papaya Soup)

5 green papayas·
2 cups chicken broth
½ teaspoon fresh ginger
 (small piece ginger
 root)

5 ounces chicken breast
½ tablespoon butter

Peel, seed and cut 1 papaya into thin 1-inch strips. Cut 1 inch from stem ends of remaining papayas and scoop out seeds with melon cutter. Set tops aside and place papayas upright in saucepan with about 2 inches of water. Simmer chicken broth and ginger 15 minutes. Cut chicken breast into thin 1-inch strips. Sauté chicken and papaya strips in butter until soft. Add to broth. Spoon mixture into prepared papayas, cover and simmer until slightly tender, about 30 minutes. Replace stem ends and serve hot. Serves 4.

LANAI TERRACE
Wailea, Hawaii • illustration by Parker Edwards

Diners have a magnificent view of the Pacific Ocean from this handsome dining room in the Inter-Continental Maui on the island of Maui. The hotel is within the 1,450-acre Wailea Resort, which includes a 36-hole championship golf complex, an 11-court tennis clubhouse, five sandy beaches and a complete program of water sports. The dining room is open for dinner and for Sunday brunch (8 a.m. to 1 p.m.). Reservations advisable for meals and rooms.

Columbia River Salmon Cardinal

Clean a 2-pound salmon filet. Make sure all bones are removed. Season to taste with salt, white pepper and lemon juice. Sauté 4 ounces sliced lobster tails and 8 ounces of shrimp. Spread cooked lobster and shrimp down the length of the salmon filet and fold ends together the long way. Wrap tightly with cheese

cloth. Tie ends securely. Poach slowly for 30-35 minutes in fish court bouillon. Set aside and make a creamy fish sauce (below) using the fish stock. Cut salmon loaf into desired portions. Cover with Creamy Fish Sauce and serve with rice. Makes 4 portions.

Creamy Fish Sauce

In a small saucepan combine 3 minced shallots with ½ cup of dry white wine. Reduce over moderate heat until liquid has evaporated. Melt 10 tablespoons butter and slowly add ½ cup flour. Stir until it makes a smooth paste. Slowly add ½ cup fish stock stirring constantly so that mixture is lump free. Simmer for 5 minutes. Add 1 ounce cognac, ½ cup cream and juice of 1 lemon. Season to taste with salt, pepper and drop of Lee & Perrins sauce. Sprinkle with parsley.

CEDARS FLOATING RESTAURANT
Coeur d'Alene, Idaho • illustration by Pete Harritos

A quarter mile south of Coeur d'Alene on U.S. 95 (about 35 miles east of Spokane), this unique glass-walled restaurant floats on Coeur d'Alene Lake and when the lake's waters rise in the spring so does the restaurant. Diners have a magnificent view of the lake and forests of fir trees set against a backdrop of mountains. Dinner only; reservations necessary. Closed on most holidays.

The Cedars Biergarten Steak Sauce

4 cups beer
1 cup soy sauce
2 teaspoons garlic
    powder
2 teaspoons ginger
    powder

Combine ingredients in a pan and heat *slowly*. Dip steaks to be broiled in the hot sauce and place on grill. Broil steaks to taste, basting them frequently with steak sauce.

Blue Cheese Dressing

1 cup sour cream
2 cups mayonnaise
Pinch of powdered garlic
Pinch of powered ginger
1 teaspoon
    Worcestershire sauce
2 ounces blue cheese,
    grated
1 teaspoon fresh lemon
    juice

Combine ingredients and blend together by hand. Let stand in a refrigerator in a covered container for 1-2 weeks before using.

THE SCHOOLHOUSE
Lakeside, Montana • illustration by Dorothy Larson

In the beautiful resort area surrounding Flathead Lake in western Montana, this lakeside dining room in a converted schoolhouse has attracted visitors from every state and Canadian province. Open for lunch and dinner and Sunday brunch. Closed all day Monday and Saturday and Sunday nights.

Reservations advisable. Open from the second Sunday in May until September 30. Jean Barry is the owner of this unique restaurant.

Sauerkraut Relish

Combine the following ingredients, all chopped fine: 1 cup onion, 2 cups celery, 1 cup green pepper, 1 cup sweet red pepper or ½ cup pimento. Add a drained, but not rinsed, No. 2½ can of sauerkraut. Mix all thoroughly in a bowl. Combine 1 cup sugar, 1 cup salad oil and ½ cup of white vinegar. Pour this mixture over sauerkraut and chill for 1 hour before serving.

EDGEWATER RESTAURANT
Missoula, Montana • illustration by Joan Solmes

From Interstate 90 take the Van Buren Street exit and follow signs to the Village Motor Inn at 100 Madison. The dining room overlooks the beautiful Clark Fork River and is across the water from the University of Montana. Overnight accommodations are available. The dining room is open from 6:30 a.m. to 10:30 p.m.

Hot Kentucky Sandwich

6 French rolls, split
18 ounces diced, cooked
    chicken meat
24 ounces cream of
    mushroom soup
6 slices American or
    Cheddar cheese
12 slices tomato
6 tablespoons grated
    Parmesan cheese
6 slices cooked bacon

Place 2 halved rolls on 6 individual sizzler plates. Sprinkle each roll half with diced chicken and cover with hot, undiluted cream of mushroom soup. Add cheese slices, then the tomato and sprinkle with grated cheese. Place 4 inches under the broiler for 5 minutes until the cheese is melted and the sandwiches are hot. Remove sandwiches to hot plates, top each with bacon slice. Serve with potato salad. Makes 6 sandwiches.

HOLE IN THE WALL
Las Vegas, Nevada • illustration by Neil Boyle

Battista Locatelli is the host at this charming Italian dining place at 4041 Audrie, in the shadow of the giant MGM Grand Hotel. Open every day for dinner, 4:30 p.m. to 10:30 p.m. Closed the last two weeks of December. "All the wine you can drink" goes with all dinners. Reservations recommended.

Veal Scaloppine

1½ pounds of veal
  scallops, sliced to
  silver dollar size (have
  butcher prepare)
1 cup flour, seasoned
  with salt and white
  pepper
2 tablespoons butter
3 tablespoons olive oil
¾ cup beef stock
2 lemons
Minced parsley

Pound veal slices with a meat cleaver, dust with flour, salt and pepper. In a skillet melt butter, add olive oil and meat, turning to brown both sides. Pour in beef stock and juice of one lemon. Cook over low heat for 5 minutes, garnish with razor thin slices of the remaining lemon, and minced parsley. Serves 4-6.

Cappucino

Combine 2 cups black coffee, 2 cups milk, 1 tablespoon sugar, 1 tablespoon dry cocoa, 1½ ounces brandy and 1½ ounces dark crème de cacao. Bring to a boil. Pour into 4 after-dinner coffee cups, top with sweetened whipped cream and a cinnamon stick.

PALACE COURT
Las Vegas, Nevada • illustration by Fred Browning

This is an oasis of quiet and elegant dining in the midst of the bustling activity at the famed Caesars Palace Hotel and Casino. The restaurant is open for lunch and dinner every day; reservations necessary. The hotel is at 3570 Las Vegas Boulevard, South, and is one block east of Interstate 15 on the Dunes-Flamingo turnoff. The hotel offers tennis, racquetball and swimming; reservations advisable for hotel accommodations.

Filet of Beef Moutarde Forestière

4 6-8 ounce beef filets,
  butterflied
6 ounces butter
6 mushrooms, sliced thin
½ teaspoon each
  rosemary and sage
¼ cup cognac
4 teaspoons Dijon
  mustard
4 teaspoons mild
  mustard
½ cup whipping cream
2 tablespoons sour
  cream
¼ teaspoon sweet
  paprika
Salt and pepper, to taste
1 tablespoon chopped
  parsley

Have all ingredients out before you start to cook. Heat two skillets, one over medium heat, one over high heat. Add 3 ounces butter to medium-hot pan; when butter is melted and hot, add mushrooms. Add remaining butter to hot pan; when butter is hot, add steaks. After a few minutes, turn steaks, then sprinkle with crushed rosemary and sage. Watch mushrooms; don't allow to burn. Push mushrooms to side. Transfer steaks to mushroom pan. Add cognac to empty pan and flame it, then add both mustards, cream and sour cream. Mix mushrooms and beef. Grate pepper over steak, and salt to taste. Sprinkle with parsley. Serve steaks piping hot topped with mustard cream sauce. Makes 4 portions.

HOLIDAY INN de LAS CRUCES
Las Cruces, New Mexico • illustration by Bruce Bond

Here you step back into territorial New Mexico atmosphere with all the authentic color of the Southwest plus the luxury of modern comforts and distinctive cuisine. The owner-manager, C. W. Ritter, has made history come alive with antiques and art forms. The inn has lavish greenery, indoor swimming pools and tiled promenades. Open for breakfast, lunch and dinner year-round. Reservations are suggested for dinner. It's at 201 East University Avenue, close to Interstate 10 and 25. The Cream of Green Chile Soup was a winner in the 1977 International Connoisseurs Chili Contest.

Cream of Green Chile Soup

¼ pound fresh long green mild chiles
2 medium bell peppers
¼ pound fresh spinach
6 tablespoons butter, divided
¼ cup chopped onion
½ small garlic clove, minced

16 oysters (canned, frozen or fresh)
2 cups hot water
6 tablespoons flour
6 cups half-and-half cream
Salt and white pepper to taste
¼ teaspoon MSG

Stem, seed and cut chiles and green peppers into pieces. Wash and tear spinach into pieces. Heat 2 tablespoons butter in saucepan. Add peppers and spinach, onion, garlic and oysters. Sauté about 10 minutes. Stir to coat well with butter and cook gently until just tender. Remove from heat and turn into blender. Add water and spin until smooth. Rub through a sieve while returning to saucepan. Set sieve with pulp aside. Heat remaining butter in another saucepan. Blend in flour to a paste. Slowly stir in cream and cook and stir over medium heat 20 minutes. Pour cream sauce through sieve into blended chile mixture. Season with salt, pepper and MSG. Cook gently 30 minutes without boiling. Garnish with chopped green chiles. Serve hot or cold. May be frozen for future use. Makes 8 bowls.

THE PALACE
Santa Fe, New Mexico • illustration by Larry McManus

Roland Menetrey has created a grand turn-of-the-century French dining room on Burro Alley in the heart of Santa Fe. The Palace is open every day from 11 a.m. to 2 a.m. except Sunday. Reservations advised for lunch and dinner.

Steak à la Diable

4 cuts of beef filet (6 ounces each)
3 teaspoons butter
4 teaspoons freshly chopped onion
1½ teaspoons freshly chopped garlic
8 ounces small mushroom caps, sliced

½ teaspoon dry English mustard
1½ teaspoons chopped chives
½ teaspoon oregano powder
1½ ounces cognac
½ cup dry white wine
3 ounces brown base sauce

Brown beef to taste. Meanwhile prepare the sauce. Simmer onion, garlic and mushrooms in butter for three minutes. Add mustard, chives and oregano. Butterfly the steaks. Place in skillet with other ingredients. Flame with cognac, add white wine, and brown base sauce. Cook for 2 minutes. Fill each steak with sauce, fold over and serve. Makes 4 portions.

Poires Belle Helene

4 stewed pear halves
4 scoops vanilla ice cream

1 pint chocolate sauce

Put scoop of ice cream in a champagne glass, place one-half pear on top and cover with hot chocolate sauce. Decorate with whipped cream. Makes 4 portions.

TINNIE'S SILVER DOLLAR
Tinnie, New Mexico • illustration by Sue T. Chapman

In 1960, the Tinnie Mercantile Company commissioned John Meigs, an artist and designer, to restore the 1892 structure that now houses this excellent restaurant. Aged beef, lamb chops, trout and quail simply prepared are the mainstays of the menu. Open daily from 5 p.m. to 11 p.m.; reservations necessary. Closed Christmas. It is on U.S. Highways 70-380 in Tinnie, which is 40 miles west of Roswell, New Mexico.

Broiled Rainbow Trout

2 14-ounce whole dressed trout	2 tablespoons finely minced parsley
2 sticks butter	⅛ teaspoon garlic powder
¼ teaspoon salt	⅛ teaspoon paprika
⅛ teaspoon freshly ground pepper	1 ounce brandy
¼ cup dry white wine	

Wash fish thoroughly with cold water. Dry with paper towels. Baste inside and outside of fish heavily with 1 butter stick melted. Season with salt and freshly ground pepper. Combine the remaining ingredients except brandy and simmer for a few minutes. Broil fish for 10 minutes on each side, basting with sauce after turning. Make sure not to overcook. Sprinkle fish with brandy and top with wine sauce before serving 4.

THE BLACK FOREST INN RESTAURANT
Bend, Oregon • illustration by Randall McKissick

Continental cuisine in a Bavarian atmosphere is a winning combination in this popular restaurant. Open for dinner every day except Monday; reservations advisable. From U.S. Highway 97, take Franklin Street to Century Drive. The restaurant is at 25 S.W. 14th Street.

Rathskeller Chicken

Pound 6 5-ounce boneless halves of chicken breasts to get an even thickness. Beat 3 eggs with 2 teaspoons water, then dust chicken breasts in 5 ounces of flour. Dip floured chicken in egg wash, then in 4 ounces cracker meal. Melt 5 ounces butter in a large fry pan and cook chicken breasts slowly (about 5 minutes each side) to a golden brown. While chicken is cooking prepare a sauce by melting 2 ounces of butter and combining with 2 ounces of flour in a 2-quart pot. Add 1 cup half and half, 1 cup milk, 6 ounces white wine, 2 tablespoons lemon juice and salt and pepper, to taste. Simmer for 5 minutes. Add 4 ounces cleaned and cooked shrimp and 2 ounces mushrooms which have been sautéed in butter. Simmer 5 minutes more, stirring occasionally. Cook 12 spears asparagus. Place chicken breasts on plate with asparagus spears on top. Top with sauce. Serve with buttered rice and vegetables. Serves 6.

VALLEY RIVER INN
Eugene, Oregon • illustration by Marcus Hamilton

Beautifully situated on the banks of the Willamette River, this elegant new motor inn is directly adjacent to Valley River Center, one of the Northwest's most complete covered mall shopping complexes. There are excellent family vacation facilities and it is also ideally suited for conventions. Breakfast, lunch and dinner served daily in the four dining rooms. Take the

Santa Clara exit from I-105 and proceed to Valley River Center.

French Onion Soup au Gratin

3 medium onions, sliced
2 tablespoons oil
1 garlic clove, chopped
3 ounces dry sherry or white wine
6 cups chicken broth
Spice bag: ½ ounce peppercorns, crushed, 1 ounce whole cloves, ¼ teaspoon thyme, 1 bay leaf tied in small linen bag

6 toasted croutons, 3 inches in diameter
5 ounces Mozzarella cheese, grated
4 ounces Swiss cheese, grated
5 ounces American cheese, grated

Sauté onions in oil over medium heat until transparent. Add garlic and wine and simmer until reduced to minimum. Add chicken broth and spice bag, simmer 15 minutes. Season to taste with salt. Remove spice bag when broth is seasoned to your taste. Pour into 6 oven-proof soup crocks. Top with toasted croutons and sprinkle with mixture of cheeses. Place under broiler until cheese is golden brown. Serves 6.

WINDWARD INN
Florence, Oregon • illustration by Robert Boston

Described by regular patrons as one of the most popular restaurants on the Oregon coast, the Inn has been a local attraction for 30 years. Present owners, Kathie and Van Heeter, have recently completed a major expansion project, which they call "coastal country inn" with a hint of Old English. Rich wood paneling and wood-burning fireplaces in the dining rooms add to the charm. The menu is wide-ranging, from local fish 'n chips to carefully prepared entrees featuring seafoods, steaks and family specialties.

Desserts are outstanding, as is the extensive wine list. Open for breakfast, lunch and dinner every day except Monday; closed Thanksgiving and Christmas. Address, 3757 U.S. Highway 101 North.

Cheese Cake

18 graham crackers
Sugar
2 teaspoons cinnamon
6 tablespoons melted butter

24 ounces cream cheese
Vanilla
4 eggs
1 pint sour cream

Roll crackers into fine crumbs. Mix with 2 tablespoons sugar, cinnamon and melted butter. Press into buttered 8-inch spring form pan. Chill while making filling. Blend cream cheese with 1 cup sugar until smooth. Blend in ½ teaspoon vanilla and eggs, one at a time. Beat thoroughly. Pour into prepared pan. Bake at 350° 40 minutes. Remove from oven and cool 20 minutes. Blend sour cream with ½ teaspoon vanilla, and 2 tablespoons sugar. Pour over cooled filling. Bake at 500° for 5 minutes. Cool then refrigerate at least 2 hours before removing from pan.

JAKE'S FAMOUS CRAWFISH
Portland, Oregon • illustration by Marcus Hamilton

One of the oldest restaurants in the state, Jake's is decorated with authentic antiques and memorabilia of the early 1900s. Regional seafood is the specialty here. Jake's is open for dinner only; reservations suggested. It is at 401 S. W. 12th Street; take 12th Street Exit from Interstate 80 or 5.

Jake's Stuffed Trout

6 8-ounce whole cleaned trout, buttered inside and out with soft butter

Shrimp Stuffing

Melt ¼ cup butter in a pan and add ¼ cup chopped onion, ½ cup chopped celery and sauté lightly, then mix with a 1-pound loaf of bread, cubed. Toss lightly and then add ½ cup dry white wine, 2 tablespoons finely chopped parsley, ½ pound raw, chopped shrimp and a raw egg. Cook over low heat for a few minutes, then mix in ½ teaspoon thyme, ½ teaspoon sage, pinch of marjoram, and salt and pepper, to taste. Add ⅓ cup chopped almonds. Remove from fire and stuff trout with mixture. Bake at 450° for 15 to 20 minutes or until golden brown. Serves 6.

SUNRIVER LODGE
Sunriver, Oregon • illustration by Richard A. Young

On the DesChutes River in central Oregon, this resort of approximately 3,300 acres offers everything from an 18-hole golf course to bike trails and cross-country skiing. There is a 4,500-foot airstrip. Breakfast, lunch and dinner served daily. Reservations necessary for dinner and accom-

modations. The lodge is 15 miles south of Bend, off U.S. Highway 97.

Poached Eggs Sunriver

8 medium sized scallops	¼ teaspoon salt
Flour	¼ pound small shrimp,
Butter	cooked and deveined
8 large eggs	Sauce Parisienne,
1 teaspoon lemon juice	(below) prepared in advance

Dredge scallops in flour. Press hard to slightly flatten. Sauté in butter. Place 2 scallops in each of 4 ceramic sea shells or individual casserole dishes. Poach eggs in water with lemon juice and salt. Place 1 egg on each scallop, then place equal amount of shrimp on each egg. Gently top with Sauce Parisienne. Set shells on plates of warm rock salt. Place under broiler 1 to 2 minutes to glaze. Serve immediately with toasted French bread. Serves 4.

Sauce Parisienne

2 tablespoons butter	Dash garlic salt
4 tablespoons flour	Salt to taste
2½ cups hot shellfish stock or 1½ cups canned clam broth plus 1 cup water	¼ cup white wine

Blend butter and flour together over medium heat. Add hot shellfish stock and garlic salt. Salt to taste and stir in wine. Cook gently until slightly thickened. Remove from heat.

ROOF RESTAURANT
Salt Lake City, Utah • illustration by Robert Boston

This new restaurant is high above downtown Salt Lake City atop the Hotel Utah. Dishes are prepared to order and all diners have a view of the city, including the historic state capitol and the illuminated spires of the famed Mormon Temple. There is piano music every evening. French chef James Ferri presides over the kitchen. Dinner is served every evening and reservations are necessary. The hotel also offers breakfast and lunch in other dining rooms and there are overnight accommodations. The hotel is downtown at Main and South Temple Streets.

Lancette of Lamb

3 pounds boneless lamb, cut into 1-inch cubes	2 tablespoons Sauterne wine
2 tablespoons light olive oil	1 cup sliced, light mushrooms
	1 cup julienne onions

4 artichoke hearts,
  quartered
¼ teaspoon minced
  garlic
Salt and pepper to taste

Cooked rice
1 tablespoon finely
  chopped parsley

Heat oil in large sauté pan. Add lamb cubes and brown on all sides. Remove lamb from pan and keep warm. Pour wine into pan, rolling around to collect pan drippings. Add mushrooms and onions, sauté 3 minutes. Add artichokes, garlic, salt and pepper to taste. Cook 1 minute. Return lamb to pan, sauté 2 minutes or until desired degree of doneness. Arrange lamb on bed of rice. Pour mushroom mixture over lamb and garnish with parsley. Serves 6 to 8.

LONGHORN BARBECUE
Spokane, Washington • illustration by Arthur Barbour

The five Lehnertz brothers own and operate this popular family restaurant. A giant smoke pit dominates the kitchen and is the source of their superb smoked ribs, hams and sausages. There is carry out service and they will travel as far as 1,000 miles to put on an authentic Western barbecue for large groups. Breakfast, lunch and dinner served daily 7 a.m. to 11 p.m. The address is Sunset Highway, Number 2.

El Rancho Beef Soup

1 pound hamburger
1 onion, chopped fine
3 stalks celery, chopped
  fine
1½ tablespoons chili
  powder
1 teaspoon cumin

1 teaspoon each: celery
  salt, onion salt and
  garlic salt
2½ cups canned red
  kidney beans
1½ quarts water

Combine ingredients and bring to a boil and let simmer for at least 15 minutes. Taste and add seasonings, if needed. Makes 10 hearty portions. Can be frozen for future use.

SPOKANE HOUSE
Spokane, Washington • illustration by Harvey Kidder

A fantastic view of the city adds to the pleasure of dining here. The Sunday morning champagne brunch is a delectable meal; at dinner, a specialty of the house is prime ribs of beef. Take the Garden Springs Exit from I-90, not far from the airport. Breakfast, lunch and dinner served daily. Reservations advisable.

Mousse au Chocolat

16 ounces semisweet
  dark chocolate
  (Baker's)
12 large eggs

2 ounces unsalted butter
1 tablespoon sugar
1 pinch salt
1 tablespoon Cointreau

Melt chocolate in a double boiler. Separate 12 eggs, add only 9 yolks. Beat whites until firm, adding the sugar in the process and at the end, the salt. Add butter to chocolate, stir until smooth, then remove from heat. Pour chocolate in a large bowl and slowly fold in, spoon by spoon, first the egg whites then the Cointreau. When mixture is finished, set in refrigerator for a few hours. Serves 10.

THE CROSSING
Vancouver, Washington • illustration by Harvey Kidder

This place, built in and around railroad cars, is a natural for railroad buffs but it has great appeal for anyone with a feeling for the nostalgia of bygone days. All dining is in vintage pullmans, coaches and diners, just a hobo's leap from the track that follows the bank of the Columbia River. Brainchild of restaurateur George Goodrich and designer Norbert Sorger, the restaurant captures the aura of the boom days of railroading. Open for lunch and dinner and Sunday morning brunch, The Crossing offers regional specialties along with steaks and roasts. Located at 900 West 7th Street, 8 blocks west of I-5.

Cheese Beer Soup

½ cup butter	3 tablespoons finely
1 cup flour	chopped green chilies
1 tablespoon salt	Dash cayenne pepper
2 quarts half and half	½ cup shredded sharp
cream, warmed	Cheddar cheese
2 cups beer, warmed	

Over low heat melt butter; blend in flour and salt. Cook to smooth paste. Gradually stir in warmed cream; cook and stir until thickened. Stir in warmed beer, chilies, cayenne and cheese. Cook over low heat until moderately thick. Serves 8.

Stuffed Zucchini

Wash and cut 4 small zucchini in halves lengthwise. Hollow out, leaving ¼ inch on all sides. Cut a thin slice from bottom of each and place on baking sheet. Blend ½ pound grated Cheddar cheese, 2 tablespoons minced parsley, 1 tablespoon clarified butter, ½ teaspoon lemon juice, ½ teaspoon granulated garlic. Fill zucchinis with mixture. Bake at 350° for 20 minutes or until bubbly. Serve on red lettuce as an appetizer or dinner vegetable. Serves 8.

MINER'S DELIGHT
Atlantic City, Wyoming • illustration by Richard A. Young

Located in a ghost town, the hotel and gourmet restaurant are housed in a turn-of-the-century stagecoach stop. The name is from the famous gold mine in the area, "Miner's Delight." It is 30 miles southwest of Lander, Wyoming, on State Highway 28. Open for dinner 6 to 11 p.m. Thursday through Sunday; reservations necessary. Closed January 1 to March 31. Overnight accommodations.

Shrimp Miner's Delight

12 ounces cooked shrimp, cut in bite-size pieces	1 tablespoon Worcestershire sauce
No. 2 can artichoke hearts	¼ cup dry sherry
12 ounces fresh mushrooms	1½ cups basic cream sauce
2 tablespoons butter	¼ cup grated Parmesan cheese
	Salt, pepper and paprika, to taste

Arrange artichoke hearts in 4 individual buttered baking dishes and place shrimp pieces over artichokes. Slice mushrooms and sauté in butter for 6 minutes and pour over shrimp. Mix Worcestershire with sherry and cream sauce, add salt and pepper, and pour over baking dishes. Sprinkle with Parmesan cheese and paprika. Bake 30-40 minutes in 375° oven. Serve hot, garnish with parsley. Serves 4 as an appetizer.

Canada

French Canadian Pea Soup – La Sapiniere, Quebec
Rhubarb Punch – Marshlands Inn, New Brunswick
Maple Syrup Pie – La Sapiniere, Quebec
Boiled Lobster – Conley's Shorehouse, New Brunswick

S. S. ESSINGTON AT THE WHARF
Vancouver, British Columbia • illustration by Bruce Bond

This delightful old sternwheeler, which once served on the Skeena and Fraser Rivers, has been turned into a floating restaurant. At 1010 Beach Avenue, at the north end of the Burrard Bridge in downtown Vancouver, this unusual dining room is open for lunch and dinner every day.

Crab Bake Imperial

1½ pounds King Crab legs
½ cup flour
3 tablespoons butter
1 teaspoon shallots, chopped fine
1 green pepper, diced
3 stalks celery, diced
1 medium onion, chopped
2 medium tomatoes, diced
½ cup dry white wine
Salt, pepper and cayenne pepper, to taste
½ teaspoon Lea & Perrins sauce
2 cups hot rice pilaf

Roll shelled crab legs in flour. Sauté crab legs in butter with the chopped vegetables. Add white wine, then season to taste with seasonings listed. Simmer until wine is reduced. Serve with rice pilaf.

Fresh Bay Scallops Essington

Boil 3 pounds fresh Bay scallops in their shells for 5-8 minutes. (Or use 1¼ pounds cooked, shelled scallops.) Remove fresh scallops from shells. Combine: ½ onion, diced, 1 teaspoon garlic, chopped fine, and 1 teaspoon shallots, chopped fine. Sauté vegetables in ¼ pound of butter until golden brown. Then add cooked scallops, 2 medium tomatoes, diced, 1 teaspoon chopped parsley and 2 ounces dry white wine. Simmer 5 minutes until done. Add salt and pepper, to taste. Serve over 2 cups hot buttered rice. Makes 4 portions.

MARSHLANDS INN
Sackville, New Brunswick • illustration by Bruce Bond

This inn was built in the early 1850s by William Crane for his daughter whose portrait hangs in the hall. Breakfast, lunch and dinner served Monday through Friday; dinner only on weekends. Closed Sunday during December and January. Reservations recommended. Overnight accommodations. The address is 73 Bridge Street. Take the first or second exit from the Trans-Canada Highway; signs then indicate direction to the inn. Mr. and Mrs. H. C. Read are the owner-managers.

Rhubarb Punch

Make rhubarb juice by boiling fresh garden rhubarb in water to cover, for about half an hour. Strain through cheesecloth. Measure juice, then add 1 cup white sugar for each cup of juice. Boil gently to a thick syrup. Use a candy thermometer to keep temperature at 210° to 215°. Bottle and keep cool. A few drops of red color may be added if rhubarb is not red. To serve fill a short glass one-third full of chilled syrup and add club soda to the top. Stir to mix. Vodka may also be added, if desired.

Buckwheat Pancakes

Mix 2 cups buckwheat, ¾ cup all-purpose flour and 1 teaspoon salt. Add about 4 cups of buttermilk and mix thoroughly to a smooth batter. Let stand overnight. When ready to serve, add 1 teaspoon soda, dissolved in a little warm water, to half of the batter. (Refrigerate remaining batter until needed.) To this half of the batter, also add enough buttermilk so that batter will pour readily. Use fat pork to grease the griddle. Set heat at 360°. Half of batter makes about 18 pancakes 4 to 5 inches in diameter. Serve with maple syrup and butter.

CONLEY'S SHOREHOUSE
St. Andrews, New Brunswick • illustration by Huntley Brown

This old-fashioned shorehouse is in the Maritimes resort community of St. Andrews at 2 Patrick Street on the water's edge. Fishing boats dock just a few feet from this restaurant with its own wholesale fish and lobster business. Open daily for lunch and dinner until 9 p.m. from May 15 to October 1.

Boiled Lobster

Fill a large kettle with water. Add 1 tablespoon salt for each quart of water. When water boils, drop in lobster head first, grasping by the middle of the back. Cover. Boil a 1- to 1½-pound lobster for 20 minutes; a 1½- to 2-pound lobster for 25 minutes. When done, lift lobster out with tongs and lay on a cutting board. Place lobster on its back. Twist off 2 large claws, then 8 small claws close to the body. Now, with the lobster still on its back, grasp its fan-tail in the left hand. Make a slit the full length of the lobster with sharp kitchen shears, starting at the tiny vent at the tail. After removing coral and liver, cut off tail shell. Carefully remove the body from the shell, discarding the small pointed sac (stomach). Arrange on platter. Serve with melted butter and lemon.

SOMEPLACE ELSE RESTAURANT
Huttonville, Ontario • illustration by Frederic Schuler Briggs

Located in a historic house which was once the residence of an 18th century Loyalist, this charming, relaxed restaurant has a uniquely satisfying atmosphere. There is country comfort with European tradition and an international menu. Lunch and dinner served every day. It is three miles north of Highway 401 (take Exit 41) on Mississauga Road in Huttonville.

Piccata Milanaise

12 slices of boneless veal, cut from leg or shoulder (about 2 pounds)	2 eggs, well beaten
	8 ounces Parmesan cheese, grated
	4 tablespoons olive oil
2 ounces flour	12 fresh apple rings
Salt and pepper, to taste	

Place veal slices between pieces of wax paper and pound slices with a thin mallet or rolling pin. Season flour with salt and pepper. Dip cutlets into flour, then into beaten eggs and finally dredge in grated cheese. Heat oil in skillet until very hot, then quickly sauté cutlets for about 2 minutes, turning once. Keep veal hot. In the same pan quickly grill apple slices on both sides and place one on each cutlet. Makes 6 servings.

Fresh Rainbow Trout, British Columbia Style

1 8-12 ounce trout	Dash tarragon
3-4 thin lemon slices	1 strip bacon (either sliced or from the side)
1 pinch pepper	
Dash garlic powder	3-4 slices onion
1 pinch red paprika	4 ounces butter

Clean trout and remove the eyes. Fill fish cavity with lemon slices. Mix pepper, garlic powder, paprika and tarragon. Sprinkle ¼ of the mixture over lemon slices. Place bacon and onion slices in trout. Sprinkle remaining spices on outside. Place fish on sheet of foil or baking paper. Top with butter, cut in pieces. Wrap fish, place on baking pan and roast in preheated 450° oven 10 to 12 minutes. Open wrap and serve in foil to enjoy the aroma that fills the room. Serves 1.

CAFE DE L'AUBERGE
Toronto, Ontario • illustration by Larry McManus

Renowned for service and cuisine, this classically elegant restaurant features Continental, classic French and native dishes. It is the main dining room of the Inn on the Park Hotel, which is 15 minutes from downtown Toronto. The address is 1100 Eglinton Avenue East. Reservations advisable.

Baked Chicken in Crust

Stuffing

Combine ¼ cup milk, 1 beaten egg, 2 teaspoons brandy and salt and pepper, to taste. Soak 6 slices white toast in this mixture. Chop 3 slices cooked bacon, 1 chicken liver and 2 green onions. Mix with 1 teaspoon chopped parsley and a pinch of thyme. Combine mixture with soaked toast and stuff cavity of a 3-pound chicken.

Crust

Mix 1½ cups all-purpose flour with ½ cup soft butter quickly with fingertips. Stir in 5 tablespoons water and a pinch of salt. Shape into a ball and let rest for 15 minutes. Then roll out thinly on a floured board. Place the chicken on its side on one half of the pastry with the breast bone towards the center of the circle. Fold over second half of the pastry to enclose the chicken. Seal the pastry along the back bone. Turn the bird breast side up and seal the ends. Place on greased baking sheet and brush the pastry with a beaten egg. Bake in a preheated 400° oven for 30 minutes and at 350° for another 30 minutes. Split crust into 2 pieces, set aside. Quarter chicken, top with stuffing and crust portion. Serves 4.

Supreme de Volaille Catherine de Rohan (Breast of Chicken)

8 chicken breasts, boned	Salt and white pepper to taste
½ cup butter	
4 ounces Canadian whiskey	¼ cup finely diced carrots
½ cup heavy cream	¼ cup finely diced celery
	Boiling water

Cut chicken breasts in half and flatten slightly by pounding between 2 sheets of waxed paper. Heat butter in large skillet, add chicken and sauté on both sides until golden brown. Remove chicken to warm serving dish and keep warm. To skillet add whiskey and cream, simmer a few minutes and season to taste with salt and white pepper. Quickly cook carrots and celery in small amount of boiling water, allowing vegetables to maintain firmness. Drain and add to cream mixture. Boil 2 minutes, then return chicken breasts to sauce. Check seasoning and heat through, about 2 minutes. Serve with rice or parsley potatoes. Serves 4.

L'HARDY'S
Toronto, Ontario • illustration by Huntley Brown

José Delgado, the executive chef at L'Hardy's, trained at the famed Spanish restaurant of the same name before starting his own establishment in Canada. There are superb sauces, soufflés and mousses as well as homemade breads and pastries. A restful European atmosphere complements the excellent service and outstanding menu. Dinner served every day, 5 to 11 p.m. except Sunday. Reservations necessary. It is located in an 80-year-old house in the Yorkville section of Toronto at 634 Church Street.

Oysters Richelieu au Pernod

24 Malpeque oysters
1½ cups milk
20 medium-size shrimp
20 scallops

12 mushroom caps
3 tablespoons butter
¼ cup Pernod
2 cups hollandaise sauce

Remove oysters from shells and poach in milk; simmer for a few minutes. Slice shrimp, scallops and mushrooms in very thin slices and sauté in butter until golden brown. Add one cup of the milk in which the oysters were poached, and let it reduce until very thick. In each oyster shell place some of the shrimp mixture, place oysters on top. Add a few drops of Pernod to each oyster: *Make sure you do not drown the flavor with too much Pernod.* Top each oyster with a little warm hollandaise sauce. Bake at 500° for 5 minutes. An appetizer for 4.

TOP HAT STEAK & LOBSTER HOUSE
Windsor, Ontario • illustration by Bruce Bond

This popular spot across the Detroit River from Detroit is noted for steaks and seafoods as well as many ethnic-oriented items. Mike Drakich, the owner, favors specialties from his native Yugoslavia. Located at 73 University Avenue, it is open for lunch and dinner every day with two live stage shows every night except Sunday.

Salata Od Paradajzo Pecenih Paprika (Tomato and Baked Pepper Salad)

1½ pounds ripe tomatoes
5 large green peppers
1 small onion, sliced (optional)

Salt and pepper
Finely chopped parsley
¼ cup oil

Dip tomatoes in boiling water for 1 minute and carefully remove skins. Slice into salad bowl. Place peppers on baking sheet and bake at 475° about 25 minutes. Place in dish, cover with towel a few minutes, then carefully slip off skins and remove seeds. Cut into long, narrow strips and mix with tomatoes and thinly sliced onion. Dust with salt and pepper, add chopped parsley and oil and chill until serving time. Serves 4 to 6.

Palacinke (Serbian Pancakes)

1 cup flour
½ teaspoon salt
1½ cups milk

3 eggs, well beaten
1 teaspoon grated lemon rind

Sift flour and salt; add milk and eggs, lemon rind and beat well. Batter should be as thick as heavy cream. Heat small skillet, grease lightly and pour in a little batter. Tilt pan back and forth to spread over bottom of pan. When brown, turn and brown on other side. Spread each pancake with jelly or cottage cheese, roll up and dust with sifted confectioners' sugar. Serves 4. (Pancakes may be browned on one side, desired filling placed on browned side, then rolled up and set aside. When ready to serve, brown lightly.)

Cevapcici (Grilled Meat Balls)

2 pounds minced beef
1 tablespoon salt

1 tablespoon pepper
Finely chopped onion (optional)

For cevapcici, according to connoisseurs, four kinds of beef must be used — from the neck, breast, shoulder and flank. But this is not imperative to enjoy this dish. Mince the meat and place it in a deep dish. Add seasonings and onion, knead like dough, mince again. Form meat into cylinders an inch in diameter and about 2 inches in length. Place on grill and broil on all sides. It takes about 15 minutes. Serve as an appetizer or a main course.

HOTEL L'ESTEREL
County Prevost, Quebec • illustration by Roy Pauli

A magnificent year-around resort on a lake in the heart of the Laurentian Mountains, L'Esterel is 51 miles north of Montreal. Take Exit 69 from Highway 15 (Laurentian Autoroute), follow 370 east for about eight miles to the hotel. Breakfast, lunch and dinner served daily in three dining rooms. Reservations advisable.

Veal Medallions Schneider

6 ounces filet of veal
Flour
3 tablespoons oil
2 shallots, chopped
1 tablespoon butter
Pinch of paprika and dry
  mustard
3 ounces brandy
½ cup white wine
½ cup brown gravy stock
Salt and pepper
8 whole scampis, shelled
1 cup concentrated veal
  stock
½ cup heavy cream
Buttered noodles

Flatten veal, cut into 4 medallions, dredge in flour and sauté in very hot oil until light brown. Remove from pan. Sauté shallots in butter until slightly colored. Add pinch of paprika, mustard, brandy, wine and gravy stock. Simmer over low heat and season to taste with salt and pepper. Add scampi, veal stock and simmer another 10 minutes. Stir in cream, add veal and remove from heat. Serve on buttered noodles. Serves 2.

Sautéed Chicken à la Grand-Mère

Quarter two chickens. Season with salt and pepper and dip chicken pieces in flour. Brown chicken in 4 tablespoons cooking oil in a skillet. Place browned chicken pieces in a casserole. To the casserole add a small piece of carrot, a stick of celery, 1 onion, diced, 1 cup red wine and 3 tablespoons chicken stock. Cook slowly in covered casserole at 350° for 45 minutes. While chicken is baking, fry ½ cup cubed salt pork and sauté ½ cup of mushroom caps in the fat. Hold. Remove chicken from the casserole gravy and strain gravy. Continue to cook gravy over medium heat until it has reached the desired consistency. Pour gravy over chicken, then add salt pork, mushrooms and ½ cup of croutons. Serves 8.

AUBERGE HANDFIELD
St. Marc, Quebec • illustration by Huntley Brown

Just a half hour from Montreal, this restaurant is in a 150-year-old house surrounded by the rich farmlands of the Richelieu River Valley. There is a marina, as well as complete vacation facilities. Breakfast, lunch and dinner served daily; reservations necessary for meals and overnight accommodations. Closed Christmas day. Take Route 20 east from Montreal, turn left onto Route 223 at Exit 112, and go six miles.

Rump of Veal Cooked in Beer

4 pounds boned rump of
  veal
2 tablespoons butter
Salt and pepper
1 onion, diced
1 carrot, diced
1 celery stalk, diced
3 bottles of beer
1 clove garlic, crushed
1 bay leaf
Thyme
1 tablespoon tomato
  paste
1 cup whipping cream

Season meat with salt and pepper. Sauté veal in butter on all sides until brown. Add vegetables and sauté for a few more minutes. Pour 2 bottles of beer over meat. Add garlic, dash of thyme, bay leaf, additional salt and pepper to taste and tomato paste. Cover and cook in 350° oven for 2 hours. Add the remaining bottle of beer gradually as the cooking juice reduces. When cooked, remove meat to a platter and keep hot. Reduce cooking juice and thicken with a mixture of 2 tablespoons of butter and 2 tablespoons of flour. Add cream. Taste for seasoning and serve sauce over veal slices.

HOTEL LE CHANTECLER
Ste. Adele, Quebec • illustration by Roy Pauli

This unique resort complex, nestled in the Laurentians at Ste. Adele, is just 42 miles north of Montreal. Winter attractions include skiing on four mountains, with 16 interlocking trails, and nine ski lifts. Snowmaking equipment guarantees snow all winter long. In the other seasons there is golf, tennis, boating, horseback riding and hiking. Vacationers enjoy fine French Canadian cuisine all year long. Meals available for nonresident guests at breakfast, lunch and dinner. Reservations necessary for overnight accommodations and meals. Take Exit 67 from Laurentian Auto Route 15.

Canadian Meat Pie (Tourtière)

1½ pounds fresh pork shoulder, medium grind	Salt and pepper, to taste
	1 bay leaf
2 medium onions, chopped	½ teaspoon nutmeg
	1½ teaspoons cinnamon
3 tablespoons butter	2 9-inch pie crusts
1 clove garlic, chopped	

Sauté onion lightly in butter and then add meat. Cook slowly on top of the stove 2½-3 hours. Meat should not be browned. The pink shade will turn a light gray. Add seasonings and mix well. Line a deep pie shell with pastry and fill with meat mixture, top with a crust. Bake in a 350° oven for 45 minutes or until pastry is a golden brown. Serves 8 main course portions.

LA SAPINIERE
Val David, Quebec • illustration by Leonard P. Johnson

This luxurious year-round resort, in the heart of the Laurentian Mountains, is 50 miles north of Montreal

by way of Autoroute 15 (Exit 47). Marcel Kretz, the chef, recently won *Chef of the Year Award*. During any season, enjoying the French Canadian cuisine at this splendid vacation spot is a favorite pastime. Breakfast, lunch and dinner reservations needed.

Cream of Mushroom Soup

Wash and chop 1¼ pounds fresh mushrooms. Chop 1 small onion and sauté in 5 tablespoons butter for 3 minutes. Add mushrooms and sauté for 5 minutes more. Stir in 5 tablespoons flour. Add 3 cups chicken broth and bring to a boil while stirring. Salt and pepper to taste. Simmer for 30 minutes. Add 1 cup coffee cream before serving. Makes 6 servings.

French Canadian Pea Soup

1 pound yellow dry peas	Small handful celery leaves
2½ quarts water	
¼ pound salt pork, cut into small pieces	A few parsley twigs
	3 bay leaves
3 onions, chopped	1 teaspoon savory
2 carrots, diced	

Pour water over peas and let stand overnight. Add remaining ingredients and bring to a boil. Simmer for 2 or 3 hours until peas are soft.

Maple Syrup Pie

1 cup maple syrup	2 tablespoons butter
⅓ cup water	½ cup pecans
3 tablespoons cornstarch	2 9-inch pie shells

Combine maple syrup and water and bring to a boil. Mix cornstarch with a little water. Mix well into boiling syrup. Stir until smooth. Add butter and nuts. Pour into pie shell and cover with top crust. Make small cuts on top crust. Bake for 20-30 minutes in a 375° oven.

Recipe Index

138

Restaurant Index

An alphabetical listing of the featured restaurants together with a reference to states and provinces in bold type. A complete listing of the restaurants by cities can be found beginning on page 5.

Ford Book and Print Offer

Ford Times Favorite Recipes, A Tribute to America and Norman Rockwell Prints

Ford Times Favorite Recipes — This all-new volume — the seventh since 1950 — is a hardcover collection of recipes and restaurant descriptions from our award-winning monthly *Ford Times* feature, "Favorite Recipes from Famous Restaurants." It even includes extra recipes for which we didn't have space in the magazine. There are 371 prized recipes from 237 restaurants. Each restaurant is illustrated with a four-color painting or photo, and information about the restaurant's location is included as a reference for travelers.

A Tribute to America — This 192-page hardcover book was produced in a limited edition as part of Ford Motor Company's 75th anniversary celebration in 1978. Most of the 37 stories are from a series on the American Revolution that appeared in *Ford Times* from July 1973 to July 1976. The stories are rich in history and drama and will delight young and old readers alike. The 56 full-color illustrations and many black-and-white drawings alone would make this volume a collector's item.

Norman Rockwell Prints — This set of four full-color prints is great for gift-giving or for your own home or office. The original paintings were commissioned by Ford Motor Company in honor of the company's 50th anniversary in 1953. The prints — each 19½ inches square on high-quality paper — are suitable for framing. The subjects are *Henry Ford as a Boy, Henry and Clara Ford With Quadricycle* (shown on coupon below), *Henry Ford in First Model A on Detroit Street* and *Model T on the Farm.*

**Ford Publications
Box 1509-B
Dearborn, Michigan 48121**

Please send me _____ copies of **Ford Times Favorite Recipes,** Volume VII, at $6.95 per copy, postpaid. Enclosed is my check payable to Ford Motor Company for $_____.

Name _____

Address _____

City _____

State _____ Zip _____

**Ford Publications
Box 1509-B
Dearborn, Michigan 48121**

Please send me _____ copies of **A Tribute to America** at $9.95 per copy, postpaid. Enclosed is my check payable to Ford Motor Company for $_____.

Name _____

Address _____

City _____

State _____ Zip _____

**Ford Publications
Box 1509-B
Dearborn, Michigan 48121**

Please send me _____ sets of four **Norman Rockwell prints** at $19.95 per set, postpaid. Enclosed is my check payable to Ford Motor Company for $_____.

Name _____

Address _____

City _____

State _____ Zip _____